RUSTY NAILS
&
ASTRONAUTS

THIS BOOK BELONGS TO:

Rusty Nails
&
Astronauts

A Wolfhound Poetry Anthology

Edited by
Robert Dunbar
&
Gabriel Fitzmaurice

Illustrated by
Marie-Louise Fitzpatrick

WOLFHOUND PRESS
Celebrating 25 *Years*

Published in 1999 by
Wolfhound Press Ltd
68 Mountjoy Square
Dublin 1, Ireland
Tel: (353-1) 874 0354
Fax: (353-1) 872 0207

The Arts Council
An Chomhairle Ealaíon

Wolfhound Press receives financial assistance from the Arts
Council/An Chomhairle Ealaíon, Dublin.

British Library Cataloguing in Publication Data
A catalogue record for this book is available from the British Library.

ISBN 0-86327-671-7 (hb)
ISBN 0-86327-781-0 (pb)

10 9 8 7 6 5 4 3 2 1

Cover illustration and design: Marie-Louise Fitzpatrick
Illustrations: Marie-Louise Fitzpatrick
Design: Wolfhound Press/Marie-Louise Fitzpatrick
Typesetting: Wolfhound Press
Printed and bound by MPG Books Ltd., Bodmin, Cornwall

Contents

For Lucy, Amy & Rory
G.F.

For Carole, Dominic & Gráinne
R.D.

Introduction

Children delight in poetry, song and rhymes; they wallow in words; they hoard words; they make up words; they pick up and play with words. Our job as poets or editors or parents or teachers is to nourish that love, to build on that need for rhythm and rhyme, for song and story.

If poetry is good for children, it is good for adults too! Much poetry crosses that boundary: adults delight in children's verse and children love much 'adult' poetry. In this anthology, we have assembled *poetry* that transcends boundaries — the child–adult boundary, the Irish-language–English-language boundary, the home–street–school boundary. Children and adults will all find something for themselves here. We see this as a *poetry* book, not a book of English-language or Irish-language verse. Too often, particularly in school, there is the Irish-language lesson, of which poetry in Irish is a part, and the English-language lesson, of which poetry in English is a part. Poetry is thus divided.

But poetry is a whole. It belongs to all languages. This is why we have presented poetry both in Irish (with translations) and English in this anthology. We have refrained from grouping the poems under subject headings as we want our readers to make their own connections. Art is democratic and we must allow our readers to react individually to poetry, to make up their own minds. A poem that is good in school should also be good at home and out on the street. Here, we hope, are poems that any child could recite anywhere and be given a hearing. Sometimes we have, for the fun of it, made obvious connections, presenting poems written in response to other poems — for instance, Nuala Ní Dhómhnaill's 'Mo Ghrása (Idir Lúibíní)' in response to Shakespeare's 'My mistress' eyes are nothing like the sun'.

Poetry is dialogue, and poets are in conversation with the whole tradition of poetry when they write. In this book we present seven hundred or so years of poetry — and not just poetry written in English. We want to present a broad canvas of poetry, some written for children, some written for adults — poetry that is as relevant today as it was when it was written, for poetry is news that stays news. The book is based soundly in Ireland, with a large representation of Irish poets drawn from the different traditions, linguistic and otherwise, on this island. There is, of course, a substantial selection from other traditions — British, European, American, Afro-American, Caribbean, Sanskrit — as well.

Childhood is an area of life that we all experience. In compiling this anthology we have both drawn, inevitably (but not exclusively), from our childhoods, one Northern Irish, the other Southern. These childhoods had many things, including poems, in common. If, as it is written, 'art discovers symmetries/Where politics must wait', this is a book that transcends boundaries; it is a book of common childhood.

Gabriel Fitzmaurice and Robert Dunbar
August 1999

The Door

Go and open the door.
Maybe outside there's
a tree, or a wood,
a garden,
or a magic city.

Go and open the door.
Maybe a dog's rummaging.
Maybe you'll see a face,
or an eye,
or the picture
of a picture.

Go and open the door.
If there's fog
it will clear.

Go and open the door.
Even if there's only
the darkness ticking,
even if there's only
the hollow wind,
even if
nothing
is there,
go and open the door.

At least
there'll be
a draught.

Miroslav Holub

Aiken Drum

There was a man lived in the moon,
and his name was Aiken Drum.
And he played upon a ladle,
and his name was Aiken Drum.

And his hat was made of good cream cheese,
and his name was Aiken Drum.
And he played upon a ladle, etc.

And his coat was made of good roast beef,
and his name was Aiken Drum.

And his buttons were made of penny loaves,
and his name was Aiken Drum.

His waistcoat was made of crust of pies,
and his name was Aiken Drum.

His breeches were made of haggis bags,
and his name was Aiken Drum.

There was a man in another town,
and his name was Willy Wood;
And he played upon a razor,
and his name was Willy Wood.

And he ate up all the good cream cheese,
and his name was Willy Wood.
And he played upon a razor, etc.

And he ate up all the good roast beef,
and his name was Willy Wood.

And he ate up all the penny loaves,
and his name was Willy Wood.

And he ate up all the good pie crust,
and his name was Willy Wood.
But he choked upon the haggis bags,
and there was an end of Willy Wood.
And he played upon a razor,
and his name was Willy Wood.

Anon

What My Lady Did

I asked my lady what she did
She gave me a silver flute and smiled.
A musician I guessed, yes that would explain
Her temperament so wild.

I asked my lady what she did
She gave me a comb inlaid with pearl.
A hairdresser I guessed, yes that would explain
Each soft and billowing curl.

I asked my lady what she did
She gave me a skein of wool and left.
A weaver I guessed, yes that would explain
Her fingers long and deft.

I asked my lady what she did
She gave me a slipper trimmed with lace.
A dancer I guessed, yes that would explain
Her suppleness and grace.

I asked my lady what she did
She gave me a picture not yet dry.
A painter I guessed, yes that would explain
The steadiness of her eye.

I asked my lady what she did
She gave me a fountain pen of gold.
A poet I guessed, yes that would explain
The strange stories that she told.

I asked my lady what she did
She told me — and oh, the grief!
I should have guessed, she's under arrest
My lady was a thief!

Roger McGough

Winter Morning

Winter is the king of showmen,
Turning tree stumps into snow men
And houses into birthday cakes
And spreading sugar over lakes.
Smooth and clean and frosty white,
The world looks good enough to bite.
That's the season to be young,
Catching snowflakes on your tongue.
Snow is snowy when it's snowing
I'm sorry it's slushy when it's going.

Ogden Nash

Mammy Said

Mammy said Mammy said
That I could paint the pavements red
Or green or white
Or black as night.

Whatever I want well I can do
As true as true
Even if
I want to sniff and sniff.

Even if
I want to live on bread and jam
Well then I can
Or live on sweets instead.
'Cause Mammy said.

Mammy said Mammy said
That I could eat my crisps in bed
Whenever I please
— With dirty knees!

And if I want to run away
And join a circus for a day
Or wear my knickers on my head
Well that's okay
'Cause Mammy said.

Margot Bosonnet

Where Go the Boats

Dark brown is the river,
Golden is the sand.
It flows along for ever,
With trees on either hand.

Green leaves a-floating,
Castles of the foam,
Boats of mine a-boating —
Where will all come home?

On goes the river
And out past the mill,
Away down the valley,
Away down the hill.

Away down the river,
A hundred miles or more,
Other little children
Shall bring my boats ashore.

Robert Louis Stevenson

River

boat-carrier
bank-lapper
home-provider
tree-reflector
leaf-catcher
field-wanderer
stone-smoother
fast-mover
gentle-stroller
sun-sparkler
sea-seeker

June Crebbin

The Old Wife and the Ghost

There was an old wife and she lived all alone
In a cottage not far from Hitchin:
And one bright night, by the full moon light,
Comes a ghost right into her kitchen.

About that kitchen neat and clean
The ghost goes pottering round.
But the poor old wife is deaf as a boot
And so hears never a sound.

The ghost blows up the kitchen fire,
As bold as bold can be;
He helps himself from the larder shelf,
But never a sound hears she.

He blows on his hands to make them warm,
And whistles aloud 'Whee-hee!'
But still as a sack the old soul lies
And never a sound hears she.

From corner to corner he runs about,
And into the cupboard he peeps;
He rattles the door and bumps on the floor,
But still the old wife sleeps.

Jangle and bang go the pots and pans,
As he throws them all around;
And the plates and mugs and dishes and jugs,
He flings them all to the ground.

Madly the ghost tears up and down
And screams like a storm at sea;
And at last the old wife stirs in her bed —
And it's 'Drat those mice,' says she.

Then the first cock crows and morning shows
And the troublesome ghost's away.
But oh! what a pickle the poor wife sees
When she gets up next day.

'Them's tidy big mice,' the old wife thinks,
And off she goes to Hitchin,
And a tidy big cat she fetches back
To keep the mice from her kitchen.

James Reeves

Who Killed Cock Robin?

Who killed Cock Robin?
I, said the Sparrow,
With my bow and arrow
I killed Cock Robin.

Who saw him die?
I, said the Fly,
With my little eye
I saw him die.

Who caught his blood?
I, said the fish,
With my little dish
I caught his blood.

Who'll make his shroud?
I, said the Beetle,
With my thread and needle
I'll make his shroud.

Who'll dig his grave?
I, said the Owl,
With my spade and trowel
I'll dig his grave.

Who'll carry him to the grave?
I, said the Kite,
If it's not in the night
I'll carry him to the grave.

Who'll carry the link?
I, said the Linnet,
I'll fetch it in a minute,
I'll carry the link.

Who'll sing a psalm?
I, said the Thrush,
As he sat on a bush,
I'll sing a psalm.

Who'll be chief mourner?
I, said the Dove,
I'll mourn for my love,
I'll be chief mourner.

Who'll be the parson?
I, said the Rook,
With my little book,
I'll be the parson.

Who'll be the clerk?
I, said the Lark,
If it's not in the dark,
I'll be the clerk.

Who'll toll the bell?
I, said the Bull,
Because I can pull,
I'll toll the bell.

All the birds in the air
Fell a-sighing and a-sobbing,
When they heard the bell toll
For poor Cock Robin.

Anon

Leaves

Who's killed the leaves?
Me, says the apple, I've killed them all.
Fat as a bomb or a cannonball
I've killed the leaves.

Who sees them drop?
Me, says the pear, they will leave me all bare
So all the people can point and stare.
I see them drop.

Who'll catch their blood?
Me, me, me, says the marrow, the marrow.
I'll get so rotund that they'll need a wheelbarrow.
I'll catch their blood.

Who'll make their shroud?
Me, says the swallow, there's just time enough
Before I must pack all my spools and be off.
I'll make their shroud.

Who'll dig their grave?
Me, says the river, with the power of the clouds
A brown deep grave I'll dig under my floods.
I'll dig their grave.

Who'll be their parson?
Me, says the crow, for it is well-known
I study the bible right down to the bone.
I'll be their parson.

Who'll be chief mourner?
Me, says the wind, I will cry through the grass
The people will pale and go cold when I pass.
I'll be chief mourner.

Who'll carry the coffin?
Me, says the sunset, the whole world will weep
To see me lower it into the deep.
I'll carry the coffin.

Who'll sing a psalm?
Me, says the tractor, with my gear grinding glottle
I'll plough up the stubble and sing through my throttle.
I'll sing the psalm.

Who'll toll the bell?
Me, says the robin, my song in October
Will tell the still gardens the leaves are over.
I'll toll the bell.

Ted Hughes

Pied Beauty

Glory be to God for dappled things —
For skies of couple-colour as a brinded cow;
For rose-moles all in stipple upon trout that swim;
Fresh-firecoal chestnut-falls; finches' wings;
Landscape plotted and pieced — fold, fallow, and plough;
And áll trádes, their gear and tackle and trim.

All things counter, original, spare, strange;
Whatever is fickle, freckled (who knows how?)
With swift, slow; sweet, sour; adazzle, dim;
He fathers-forth whose beauty is past change:
      Praise him.

Gerard Manley Hopkins

Two Tongue Twisters

A canner exceedingly canny
One morning remarked to his granny,
'A canner can can
Anything that he can,
But a canner can't can a can, can he?'

A tutor who tooted the flute
Tried to tutor two tooters to toot.
Said the two to the tutor,
'Is it harder to toot, or
To tutor two tooters to toot?'

Carolyn Wells

The Cow

The Cow is of the bovine ilk;
One end is moo, the other milk.

Ogden Nash

W

The King sent for his wise men all
To find a rhyme for W.
When they had thought a good long time
But could not think of a single rhyme,
'I'm sorry,' said he, 'to trouble you.'

James Reeves

When I Was Three

When I was three I had a friend
Who asked me why bananas bend,
I told him why, but now I'm four
I'm not so sure...

Richard Edwards

Tall Paul

When I was small, they'd smile and say:
'Don't worry, Paul, that's just the way
You're built; you'll grow up tall one day.'

But now I'm grown and *seven feet* tall,
They smile and say: 'Don't worry, Paul,
Er . . . have you thought of basketball?'

Richard Edwards

? ? ?

'I've lately discovered,' the Prof said to Ron,
'That monkeys are people with overcoats on.'
'But how do you know,' answered Ron to the Prof,
'That people aren't monkeys with overcoats off?'

Richard Edwards

I'm a Grown Man Now

I'm a grown man now
Don't easily scare
(If you don't believe me
ask my teddy bear).

Roger McGough

Insides

I'm very grateful to my skin
For keeping all my insides in —
I do so hate to think about
What I would look like inside-out.

Colin West

William Caxton

William Caxton's eyes were glinting.
The glorious day he started printing.
The prospect might have pleased him less,
If he'd foreseen the Tabloid Press.

Gordon Snell

Ben

Ben's done something really bad,
He's forged a letter from his dad.
He's scrawled:
Dear Miss,
Please let Ben be
Excused this week from all P.E.
He's got a bad cold in his chest
And so I think it might be best
If he throughout this week could be
Excused from doing all P.E.
I hope my writing's
not too bad.
Yours sincerely
(signed) Ben's Dad

Colin West

The Human Beanpole

The thinnest man I ever saw
Was called 'the human beanpole'.
He'd never open any door,
But slip in through the keyhole!

Colin McNaughton

A Smile

Smiling is infectious,
you catch it like the flu.
When someone smiled at me today
I started smiling too.

I passed around the corner
and someone saw my grin.
When he smiled, I realised
I'd passed it on to him.

I thought about my smile and then
I realised its worth.
A single smile like mine could travel
right around the earth.

If you feel a smile begin
don't leave it undetected
Let's start an epidemic quick
and get the world infected.

Jez Alborough

Jim

who ran away from his Nurse, and was eaten by a Lion

There was a Boy whose name was Jim;
His Friends were very good to him.
They gave him Tea, and Cakes, and Jam,
And slices of delicious Ham,
And Chocolate with pink inside,
And little Tricycles to ride,
And read him Stories through and through,
And even took him to the Zoo —
And there it was the dreadful Fate
Befell him, which I now relate.
You know — at least you ought to know,
For I have often told you so —
That Children never are allowed
To leave their Nurses in a Crowd;
Now this was Jim's especial Foible,
He ran away when he was able,
 And on this inauspicious day
He slipped his hand and ran away!
He hadn't gone a yard when —
    Bang!
With open Jaws, a Lion sprang,
And hungrily began to eat
The Boy; beginning at his feet.
Now just imagine how it feels
When first your toes and then your heels,
And then by gradual degrees,
Your shins and ankles, calves and knees,
Are slowly eaten, bit by bit.

No wonder Jim detested it!
No wonder that he shouted 'Hi!'
The Honest Keeper heard his cry,
Though very fat he almost ran
To help the little gentleman.

'Ponto!' he ordered, as he came
(For Ponto was the Lion's name),
'Ponto!' he cried,with angry Frown.
'Let go, Sir! Down, Sir! Put it down!'
The Lion made a sudden Stop,
He let the Dainty Morsel drop,
And slunk reluctant to his Cage,
Snarling with Disappointed Rage.
But when he bent him over Jim
The Honest Keeper's
Eyes were dim.
The Lion having reached his Head,
The Miserable Boy was dead!

When Nurse informed his Parents, they
Were more Concerned than I can say:—
His Mother, as she dried her eyes,
Said, 'Well — it gives me no surprise,
He would not do as he was told!'
His Father, who was self-controlled,
Bade all the children round attend
To James' miserable end,
And always keep a-hold of Nurse
For fear of finding something worse.

Hilaire Belloc

Kenneth

who was too fond of bubble-gum and met an untimely end

The chief defect of Kenneth Plumb
Was chewing too much bubble-gum.
He chewed away with all his might,
Morning, evening, noon and night.
Even (oh, it makes you weep)
Blowing bubbles in his sleep.
He simply couldn't get enough!
His face was covered with the stuff.
As for his teeth — oh, what a sight!
It was a wonder he could bite.
His loving mother and his dad
Both remonstrated with the lad.
Ken repaid them for the trouble
By blowing yet another bubble.

Twas no joke. It isn't funny
Spending all your pocket money
On the day's supply of gum —
Sometimes Kenny felt quite glum.
As he grew, so did his need —
There seemed no limit to his greed:
At ten he often put away
Ninety-seven packs a day.

Then at last he went too far —
Sitting in his father's car,
Stuffing gum without a pause,
Found that he had jammed his jaws.
He nudged his dad and pointed to
The mouthful that he couldn't chew.
'Well, spit it out if you can't chew it!'
Ken shook his head. He couldn't do it.
Before long he began to groan —
The gum was solid as a stone.
Dad took him to a builder's yard;
They couldn't help. It was too hard.
They called a doctor and he said,
'This silly boy will soon be dead.
His mouth's so full of bubble-gum
No nourishment can reach his tum.'

Remember Ken and please do not
Go buying too much you-know-what.

Wendy Cope

Mr Fox

A Fox started out in a hungry plight,
And begged of the moon to give him light,
For he'd a long way to go that night
Before he could reach the downs, O!
Downs, O! Downs, O!
For he'd a long way to go that night
Before he could reach the downs, O!

The Fox when he came to the farmer's gate,
What should he see but the farmer's black duck!
'I love you,' says he, 'for your master's sake,
And I long to be picking your bones, O!
Bones, O! Bones, O!
I love you,' says he, 'for your master's sake,
And I long to be picking your bones, O!'

Then he seized the black duck by the neck,
And swung her all across his back,
The black duck cried out, 'Quack! Quack! Quack!'
With her legs hanging dangling down, O!
Down, O! Down, O!
The black duck cried out, 'Quack! Quack! Quack!'
With her legs hanging dangling down, O!

Old Mother Slipper-slopper jumped out of bed,
And out of the window she popped her old head,
Crying, 'John, John, John, the black duck is gone,
And the Fox has run off to his den, O!
Den, O! Den, O!
John, John, John, the black duck is gone,
And the Fox has run off to his den, O!'

Then John, he went up to the top of the hill,
And blew his horn both loud and shrill.
Says the Fox, 'That is very pretty music, still
I'd rather be safe in my den, O!
Den, O! Den, O!'
Says the Fox, 'That is very pretty music, still
I'd rather be safe in my den, O!'

At last Mr. Fox got home to his den,
To his dear little foxes, eight, nine, ten,
Says he, 'We're in luck, here's a fine fat duck,
With her legs all dangling down, O!
Down, O! Down, O!'
Says he, 'We're in luck, here's a fine fat duck,
With her legs all dangling down, O!'

Then the Fox sat down with his cubs and his wife;
They did very well without fork and knife,
Nor ate a better duck in all their life,
And the little ones picked the bones, O!
Bones O! Bones O!
They never ate a better duck in all their life,
And the little ones picked the bones, O!

Mother Goose

37

Kite

I'm
part of a
project on flight.
I'm supposed to attain
a great height. But
unfortunately
I got stuck
in a tree
so
it looks
like
I'm
here
for
the
night!

June Crebbin

Whether

Whether the weather be fine
Or whether the weather be not
Whether the weather be cold
Or whether the weather be hot —
We'll weather the weather
Whatever the weather
Whether we like it or not!

Anon

The Rainbow

The rainbow's like a coloured bridge
that sometimes shines from ridge to ridge.
Today one end is in the sea,
the other's in this field with me.

Iain Crichton-Smith

Sumer[1] Is Icumen In

Sumer is icumen in,
Lhude[2] sing cuccu!
Groweth seed and bloweth meed
And springeth the wode[3] nu.[4]
Sing cuccu!

Awe[5] bleteth after lomb,[6]
Lhouth[7] after calve cu,[8]
Bulloc[9] sterteth, bucke farteth.
Murie sing cuccu!
Cuccu, cuccu,
Well singes thu[10] cuccu.
Ne swik thu navar nu![11]

Sing cuccu nu, Sing cuccu!
Sing cuccu,
Sing cuccu nu!

Anon

1. sumer: Summer   2. Lhude: Loud

7. Lhouth: i.e. Loweth   6. lomb: lamb   5. Awe: Ewe   4. nu: now   3. Wode: Wood

8. cu: cow   9. Bulloc: Bullock   10. thu: i.e. thou   11. Ne swik thu naver nu: don't ever stop

Ancient Music

Winter is icummen in,
Lhude sing Goddamm,
Raineth drop and staineth slop,
And how the wind doth ramm!
Sing: Goddamm.
Skiddeth bus and sloppeth us,
An ague hath my ham.
Freezeth river, turneth liver,
Damn you, sing: Goddamm.
Goddamm, Goddamm, 'tis why I am, Goddamm,
So 'gainst the winter's balm.
Sing goddamm, damm, sing goddamm,
Sing goddamm, sing goddamm, DAMM

Ezra Pound

When Icicles Hang by the Wall

When icicles hang by the wall,
And Dick the shepherd blows his nail.[1]
And Tom bears logs into the hall,
And milk comes frozen home in pail,
When blood is nipp'd,[2] and ways be foul,[3]
Then nightly sings the staring owl,
To-whit!
To-who! — a merry note,
While greasy Joan doth keel[4] the pot.

When all aloud the wind doth blow,
And coughing drowns the parson's saw[5]
And birds sit brooding in the snow,
And Marian's nose looks red and raw,
When roasted crabs hiss in the bowl,
Then nightly sings the staring owl,
To-whit!
To-who! — a merry note,
While greasy Joan doth keel the pot.

William Shakespeare

1. blows his nail: breathes on his benumbed finger tips
2. nipped: chilled, stung with the cold
3. ways to be foul: roads are muddy
4. keel: keep the pot from boiling over by scumming it
5. saw: sermon

Winter Song

When Blizzards blow under the tiles
And the dishcloth crisps on the draining-board
And the snowscape stretches for miles and miles
And only the idiot ventures abroad.
When it's early to bed, and thank heavens for that,
Then coldly keens the cast-out cat:
Miaow! Miaow! — a doleful din
And who will rise and let him in?

When slippery stones by the pond
Make filling a bucket an effort of will
And you're walled-up for weeks in the back of beyond
In a farm at the foot of a hell of a hill
Then it's early to bed, and thank heavens for that,
Till coldly keens the cast-out cat:
Miaow! Miaow! — a doleful din
And who will rise and let him in?

Ann Drysdale

43

For Them

Before you bid, for Christmas' sake,
Your guests to sit at meat,
Oh please to save a little cake
For them that have no treat.

Before you go down party-dressed
In silver gown or gold,
Oh please to send a little vest
To them that still go cold.

Before you give your girl and boy
Gay gifts to be undone,
Oh please to spare a little toy
To them that will have none.

Before you gather round the tree
To dance the day about,
Oh please to give a little glee
To them that go without.

Eleanor Farjeon

little tree

little tree
little silent Christmas tree
you are so little
you are more like a flower

who found you in the green forest
and were you very sorry to come away?
see i will comfort you
because you smell so sweetly

i will kiss your cool bark
and hug you safe and tight
just as your mother would,
only don't be afraid

look the spangles
that sleep all the year in a dark box
dreaming of being taken out and allowed to shine,
the balls the chains red and gold the fluffy threads,

put up your little arms
and i'll give them all to you to hold
every finger shall have its ring
and there won't be a single place dark or unhappy

then when you're quite dressed
you'll stand in the window for everyone to see
and how they'll stare!
oh but you'll be very proud

and my little sister and i will take hands
and looking up at our beautiful tree
we'll dance and sing
'Noel Noel'

E.E. Cummings

Three Rusty Nails

Mother, there's a strange man
Waiting at the door
With a familiar sort of face
You feel you've seen before.

Says his name is Jesus
Can we spare a couple of bob
Says he's been made redundant
And now can't find a job.

Yes I think he is a foreigner
Egyptian or a Jew
Oh aye, and that reminds me
He'd like some water too.

Well shall I give him what he wants
Or send him on his way?
O.K. I'll give him 5p
Say that's all we've got today.

And I'll forget about the water
I suppose it's a bit unfair
But honest, he's filthy dirty
All beard and straggly hair.

Mother, he asked about the water
I said the tank had burst
Anyway I gave him the coppers
That seemed to quench his thirst.

He said it was little things like that
That kept him on the rails
Then he gave me his autographed picture
And these three rusty nails.

Roger McGough

In the Stable: Christmas Haiku

Donkey
My long ears can hear
Angels singing, but my song
Would wake the baby.

Dog
I will not bark but
Lie, head on paws, eyes watching
All these visitors.

Cat
I will wash my feet. For
This baby all should be clean.
My purr will soothe him.

Owl
My round eyes look down.
No starlit hunting this night:
Peace to little ones!

Spider
My fine web sparkles:
Indoor star in the roof's night
Over the baby.

Michael Harrison

Oíche Nollag

Le coinnle na n-aingeal tá an spéir amuigh breactha,
Tá fiacail an tseaca sa ghaoith ón gcnoc,
Adaigh an tine is téir chun na leapan,
Luídfidh Mac Dé ins an tigh seo anocht.

Fágaidh an doras ar leathadh ina coinne,
An mhaighdean a thiocfaidh is a naí ar a hucht,
Deonaigh do shuaimhneas a ligint, a Mhuire,
Luíodh Mac Dé ins an tigh seo anocht.

Bhí soilse ar lasadh i dtigh sin na haíochta,
Cóiriú gan caoile, bia agus deoch,
Do cheannaithe olla, do cheannaithe síoda,
Ach luífidh Mac Dé ins an tigh seo anocht.

Máire Mhac an tSaoi

Christmas Eve

With candles of angels the sky is now dappled,
The frost on the wind from the hills has a bite,
Kindle the fire and go to your slumber
Jesus will lie in this household tonight.

Leave all the doors wide open before her,
The Virgin who'll come with the child on her breast,
Grant that you'll stop here tonight, Holy Mary,
That Jesus tonight in this household may rest.

The lights were all lighting in that little hostel,
There were generous servings of victuals and wine
For merchants of silk, for merchants of woollens,
But Jesus will lie in this household tonight.

'Oíche Nollag' translated
by Gabriel Fitzmaurice

A Christmas Childhood

I

One side of the potato-pits was white with frost —
How wonderful that was, how wonderful!
And when we put our ears to the paling-post
The music that came out was magical.

The light between the ricks of hay and straw
Was a hole in Heaven's gable. An apple tree
With its December-glinting fruit we saw —
O you, Eve, were the world that tempted me

To eat the knowledge that grew in clay
And death the germ within it! Now and then
I can remember something of the gay
Garden that was childhood's. Again

The tracks of cattle to a drinking-place,
A green stone lying sideways in a ditch
Or any common sight the transfigured face
Of a beauty that the world did not touch.

II

My father played the melodeon
Outside at our gate:
There were stars in the morning east
And they danced to his music.

Across the wild bogs his melodeon called
To Lennons and Callans.
As I pulled on my trousers in a hurry
I knew some strange thing had happened.

Outside the cow-house my mother
Made the music of milking;
The light of her stable-lamp was a star
And the frost of Bethlehem made it twinkle.

A water-hen screeched in the bog,
Mass-going feet
Crunched the wafer-ice on the pot-holes,
Somebody wistfully twisted the bellows wheel.

My child poet picked out the letters
On the grey stone,
In silver the wonder of a Christmas townland,
The winking glitter of a frosty dawn.

Cassiopeia was over
Cassidy's hanging hill,
I looked and three whin bushes rode across
The horizon — the Three Wise Kings.

An old man passing said:
'Can't he make it talk' —
The melodeon. I hid in the doorway
And tightened the belt of my box-pleated coat.

I nicked six nicks on the door-post
With my penknife's big blade —
There was a little one for cutting tobacco.
And I was six Christmases of age.

My father played the melodeon,
My mother milked the cows,
And I had a prayer like a white rose pinned
On the Virgin Mary's blouse.

Patrick Kavanagh

Sir Patrick Spens

I. The Sailing

The king sits in Dunfermline town
Drinking the blude[1]-red wine;
'O whare will I get a skeely[2] skipper
To sail this new ship o' mine?'

O up and spak[3] an eldern[4] knight,
Sat at the king's right knee;
'Sir Patrick Spens is the best sailor
That ever sail'd the sea.'

Our king has written a braid[5] letter,
And seal'd it with his hand,
And sent it to Sir Patrick Spens,
Was walking on the strand.

'To Noroway, to Noroway,
To Noroway o'er the faem;[6]
The king's daughter o'Noroway,
'Tis thou must bring her hame.'[7]

The first word that Sir Patrick read
So loud, loud laugh'd he;
The neist[8] word that Sir Patrick read
The tear blinded his e'e.[9]

1. blude: blood   2. skeely: skilful   3. spak: spake (spoke)   4. eldern: oldish   5. braid: plain, outspoken   6. faem: foam   7. hame: home   8. neist: next   9. e'e: eye   10. wha: who   11. weet: wee   12. hoysed: hoisted   13. Monenday: Monday   14. may: were capable of   15. Wodensday: Wednesd

'O wha[10] is this has done this deed
And tauld the king o' me,
To send us out, at this time o' year,
To sail upon the sea?

'Be it wind, be it weet,[11] be it hail, be it sleet
Our ship must sail the faem;
The king's daughter o' Noroway
'Tis we must fetch her hame.'

They hoysed[12] their sails on Monenday[13] morn
Wi' a' the speed they may;[14]
They hae landed in Noroway
Upon a wodensday.[15]

II. The Return

'Mak[16] ready, mak ready, my merry men a'![17]
Our gude[18] ship sails the morn.'
'Now ever alack, my master dear,
I fear a deadly storm.

'I saw the new moon late yestreen[19]
Wi'[20] the auld moon in her arm;
And if we gang[21] to sea, master,
I fear we'll come to harm.'

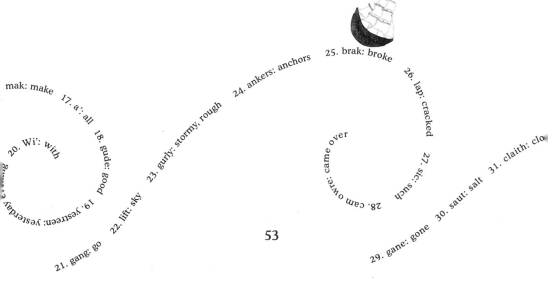

mak: make
17. a': all
18. gude: good
19. yestreen: yesterday
20. Wi': with
21. gang: go
22. lift: sky
23. gurly: stormy, rough
24. ankers: anchors
25. brak: broke
26. lap: cracked
27. sic: such
28. cam owre: came over
29. gane: gone
30. saut: salt
31. claith: clo

53

They hadna sail'd a league, a league,
A league, but barely three,
When the lift[22] grew dark, and the wind blew loud
And gurly[23] grew the sea.

The ankers[24] brak,[25] and the topmast lap,[26]
It was sic[27] a deadly storm:
And the waves cam owre[28] the broken ship
Till a' her sides were torn.

'O where will I get a gude sailor
To tak' my helm in hand,
Till I get up to the tall topmast
To see if I can spy land?'

'O here am I, a sailor gude,
To tak' the helm in hand,
Till you go up to the tall topmast,
But I fear you'll ne'er spy land.'

He hadna gane[29] a step, a step,
A step but barely ane,
When a bolt flew out of our goodly ship,
And the saut[30] sea it came in.

'Go fetch a web o' the silken claith,[31]
Another o' the twine,[32]
And wap[33] them into our ship's side,
And let nae the sea come in.'

29. gane: gone 30. saut: salt 31. claith: cloth 32. twine: string, twisted thread 33. wap: thrust quickly, pack forcibly 34. laith: reluctant 35. cork-heeled shoon: high-heeled shoes

They fetch'd a web o' the silken claith,
Another o' the twine,
And they wapp'd them round that gude ship's side,
But still the sea came in.

O laith,[34] laith were our gude Scots lords
To wet their cork-heel'd shoon;[35]
But lang or[36] a' the play was play'd
They wat[37] their hats aboon.[38]

And mony[39] was the feather bed
That flatter'd[40] on the faem;
And mony was the gude lord's son
That never mair[41] cam hame.

O lang,[42] lang may the ladies sit,
Wi' their fans into their hand,
Before they see Sir Patrick Spens
Come sailing to the strand!

And lang, lang may the maidens sit
Wi' their gowd[43] kames[44] in their hair
A-waiting for their ain[45] dear loves!
For them they'll see nae mair.

Half owre,[46] half owre to Aberdour
'Tis fifty fathoms deep;
And there lies gude Sir Patrick Spens
Wi' the Scots lords at his feet!

Traditional

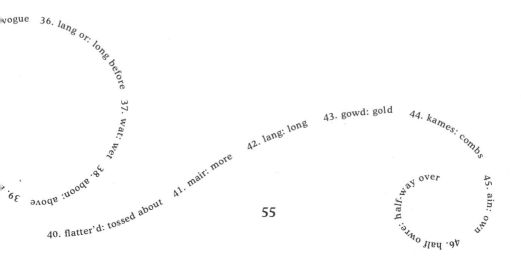

vogue   36. lang or: long before   37. wat: wet   38. aboon: above   39. ...   40. flatter'd: tossed about   41. mair: more   42. lang: long   43. gowd: gold   44. kames: combs   45. ain: own   46. half owre: half-way over

Claudy

for Harry Barton, a song

The Sperrins surround it, the Faughan flows by,
at each end of Main Street the hills and the sky,
the small town of Claudy at ease in the sun
last July in the morning, a new day begun.

How peaceful and pretty if the moment could stop,
McIlhenny is straightening things in his shop,
and his wife is outside serving petrol, and then
a girl takes a cloth to a big window pane.

And McCloskey is taking the weight off his feet,
and McClelland and Miller are sweeping the street,
and, delivering milk at the Beaufort Hotel,
young Temple's enjoying his first job quite well.

And Mrs McLaughlin is scrubbing her floor,
and Artie Hone's crossing the street to a door,
and Mrs Brown, looking around for her cat,
goes off up an entry — what's strange about that?

Not much — but before she comes back to the road
that strange car parked outside her house will explode,
and all of the people I've mentioned outside
will be waiting to die or already have died.

An explosion too loud for your eardrums to bear,
and young children squealing like pigs in the square,
and all faces chalk-white and streaked with bright red,
and the glass and the dust and the terrible dead.

56

For an old lady's legs are ripped off, and the head
of a man's hanging open, and still he's not dead.
He is screaming for mercy, and his son stands and stares
and stares, and then suddenly, quick, disappears.

And Christ, little Katherine Aiken is dead
and Mrs McLaughlin is pierced through the head.
Meanwhile to Dungiven the killers have gone,
and they're finding it hard to get through on the phone.

James Simmons

The Listeners

'Is there anybody there?' said the Traveller,
Knocking on the moonlit door;
And his horse in the silence champed the grasses
Of the forest's ferny floor:
And a bird flew out of the turret,
Above the Traveller's head:
And he smote upon the door a second time;
'Is there anybody there?' he said.
But no one descended to the Traveller;
No head from the leaf-fringed sill
Leaned over and looked into his grey eyes,
Where he stood perplexed and still.
But only a host of phantom listeners
That dwelt in the long house then
Stood listening in the quiet of the moonlight
To that voice from the world of men:
Stood thronging the faint moonbeams on the dark stair,
That goes down to the empty hall,
Hearkening in an air stirred and shaken
By the lonely Traveller's call.
And he felt in his heart their strangeness,
Their stillness answering his cry,
While his horse moved, cropping the dark turf,
'Neath the starred and leafy sky;
For he suddenly smote on the door, even
Louder, and lifted his head:
'Tell them I came, and no one answered,
That I kept my word,' he said.
Never the least stir made the listeners
Though every word he spake
Fell echoing through the shadowiness of the still house
From the one man left awake:
Ay, they heard his foot upon the stirrup,
And the sound of iron on stone,
And how the silence surged softly backward,
When the plunging hoofs were gone.

Walter De La Mare

Crab Apple Jelly

Every year you said it wasn't worth the trouble —
you'd better things to do with your time —
and it made you furious when the jars
were sold at the church fête
for less than the cost of the sugar.

And every year you drove into the lanes
around Calverton to search
for the wild trees whose apples
looked as red and as sweet as cherries,
and tasted sourer than gooseberries.

You cooked them in the wide copper pan
Grandma brought with her from Wigan,
smashing them against the sides
with a long wooden spoon to split
the skins, straining the pulp

through an old muslin nappy.
It hung for days, tied with string
to the kitchen steps, dripping
into a bowl on the floor—
brown-stained, horrible,

a head in a bag, a pouch
of sourness, of all that went wrong
in that house of women. The last drops
you wrung out with your hands;
then, closing doors and windows
to shut out the clamouring wasps,
you boiled up the juice with sugar,
dribbling the syrup onto a cold plate
until it set to a glaze,
filling the heated jars.

When the jars were cool
you held one up to the light
to see if the jelly had cleared.
Oh Mummy, it was as clear and shining
as stained glass and the colour of fire.

Vicki Feaver

O What is that Sound

O what is that sound which so thrills the ear
Down in the valley drumming, drumming?
Only the scarlet soldiers, dear,
The soldiers coming.

O what is that light I see flashing so clear
Over the distance brightly, brightly?
Only the sun on their weapons, dear,
As they step lightly.

O what are they doing with all that gear,
What are they doing this morning, this morning?
Only their usual manoeuvres, dear,
Or perhaps a warning.

O why have they left the road down there,
Why are they suddenly wheeling, wheeling?
Perhaps a change in their orders, dear.
Why are you kneeling?

O haven't they stopped for the doctor's care,
Haven't they reined their horses, their horses?
Why, they are none of them wounded, dear,
None of these forces.

O is it the parson they want, with white hair,
Is it the parson, is it, is it?
No, they are passing his gateway, dear,
Without a visit.

O it must be the farmer who lives so near.
It must be the farmer so cunning, so cunning?
They have passed the farmyard already, dear,
And now they are running.

O where are you going? Stay with me here!
Were the vows you swore deceiving, deceiving?
No, I promised to love you, dear,
But I must be leaving.

O it's broken the lock and splintered the door,
O it's the gate where they're turning, turning;
Their boots are heavy on the floor
And their eyes are burning.

W.H. Auden

Stopping by Woods on a Snowy Evening

Whose woods these are I think I know.
His house is in the village though;
He will not see me stopping here
To watch his woods fill up with snow.

My little horse must think it queer
To stop without a farmhouse near
Between the woods and frozen lake
The darkest evening of the year.

He gives his harness bells a shake
To ask if there is some mistake.
The only other sound's the sweep
Of easy wind and downy flake.

The woods are lovely, dark and deep,
But I have promises to keep,
And miles to go before I sleep,
And miles to go before I sleep.

Robert Frost

The Runaway

Once when the snow of the year was beginning to fall,
We stopped by a mountain pasture to say 'Whose colt?'
A little Morgan had one forefoot on the wall,
The other curled at his breast. He dipped his head
And snorted to us. And then he had to bolt.
We heard the miniature thunder where he fled,
And we saw him, or thought we saw him, dim and grey,
Like a shadow against the curtain of falling flakes.
'I think the little fellow's afraid of the snow.
He isn't winter-broken. It isn't play
With the little fellow at all. He's running away.
I doubt if even his mother could tell him, "Sakes,
It's only weather." He'd think she didn't know!
Where is his mother? He can't be out alone.'
And now he comes again with clatter of stone,
And mounts the wall again with whited eyes
And all his tail that isn't hair up straight.
He shudders his coat as if to throw off flies.
'Whoever it is that leaves him out so late,
When other creatures have gone to stall and bin,
Ought to be told to come and take him in.'

Robert Frost

from The Deserted Village

Sweet smiling village, loveliest of the lawn,
Thy sports are fled, and all thy charms withdrawn;
Admidst thy bowers the tyrant's hand is seen,
And desolation saddens all thy green:
One only master graps the whole domain,
And half a tillage stints thy smiling plain.
No more thy glassy brook reflects the day,
But, choked with sedges, works its weedy way;
Along thy glades, a solitary guest,
The hollow-sounding bittern guards its nest;
Amidst thy desert walks the lapwing flies,
And tires their echoes with unvaried cries;
Sunk are thy bowers in shapeless ruin all,
And the long grass o'ertops the mouldering wall;
And trembling, shrinking from the spoiler's hand,
Far, far away thy children leave the land.

Ill fares the land, to hastening ills a prey,
Where wealth accumulates, and men decay:
Princes and lords may flourish, or may fade;
A breath can make them, as a breath has made:
But a bold peasantry, their country's pride,
When once destroyed, can never be supplied.

Oliver Goldsmith

The Deserted Village

We came over the mountain
And found a village of secrets.

A street, a church, a school,
A village green.
But all we could hear was silence.
No children, no people,
No bleating of sheep on the hills
Or cackle of rooks in the trees,
No bells from the church.

No smoke from the chimneys
And the windows were watching eyes.
We crept closer and peered in
And saw that the rooms were bare
No food on the tables,
No fires in the hearths.

There were seats on the green
But where were the old folk with stories to tell
And where were the children with games to play?
Or the wives and the fathers, where were they?

We wanted to shout out and shatter the silence
But it clutched at our tongues,
It clutched at our hearts
And we walked on into the darkening day
And down to the valley, miles away.

Berlie Doherty

Train by Skerries

The Mourne Mountains a blue crinkle in the haze
Our train flickered by, running a dog along the
Railings, its shadow barking after us.
Children on the beach waved and one, just one jumped,
Folding her legs under her, suspended in my mind for ever,
Hair streaming goodbye as she shot behind a martello tower.
Beside me a nun reading and a priest reading
And the feeling that there was an ending and beginning,
Here in all meeting, the child hung on a moment
And the eternal sea falling on the shore was all
And the child still hung upon the air was all
And the broom, burning in the late May sun was all, was all.

Mike Harding

First Primrose

I saw it in the lane
One morning going to school
After a soaking night of rain,
The year's first primrose,
Lying there familiar and cool
In its private place
Where little else grows
Beneath dripping hedgerows,
Stalk still wet, face
Pale as Inca gold,
Spring glistening in every delicate fold.
I knelt down by the roadside there,
Caught the faint whiff of its shy scent
On the cold and public air,
Then got up and went
On my slow way,
Glad and grateful I'd seen
The first primrose of that day,
Half yellow, half green.

Leonard Clark

Useless Things

A spout without a hole
A Swiss without a roll
Ladders without rungs
Taste without tongues,

A shepherd without sheep
A horn without a beep
Hockey without sticks
Candles without wicks,

A pier without the sea
A buzz without a bee
A lid without a box
Keys without locks,

A harp without a string
A pong without a ping
A broom without its bristles
Refs without whistles,

A glacier without ice
Ludo without dice
A chair without a seat
Steps without feet,

A hat without a head
A toaster without bread
A riddle without a clue
Me without you.

Richard Edwards

Meg Merrilies

Old Meg she was a Gipsy
And liv'd upon the Moors:
Her bed it was the brown heath turf,
And her house was out of doors.

Her apples were swart blackberries,
Her currants pods o' broom;
Her wine was dew o' the wild white rose
Her book a churchyard tomb.

Her Brothers were the craggy hills,
Her Sisters larchen trees —
Alone with her great family
She liv'd as she did please.

No breakfast had she many a morn,
No dinner many a noon,
And 'stead of supper she would stare
Full hard against the Moon.

But every morn of woodbine fresh
She made her garlanding,
And every night the dark glen Yew
She wove, and she would sing.

And with her fingers old and brown
She plaited Mats o'Rushes,
And gave them to the Cottagers
She met among the Bushes.

Old Meg was brave as Margaret Queen
And tall as Amazon:
An old red blanket cloak she wore;
A chip hat had she on.
God rest her aged bones somewhere —
She died full long agone!

John Keats

69

The Stones

Worried mothers bawled her name
To call wild children from their games.

'Nellie Mulcahy! Nellie Mulcahy!
If ye don't come home,
She'll carry ye off in her big black bag.'

Her name was fear and fear begat obedience,
But one day she made a real appearance —
A harmless hag with a bag on her back.
When the children heard, they gathered together
And in a trice were
Stalking the little weary traveller —
Ten, twenty, thirty, forty.
Numbers gave them courage
Though, had they known it,
Nellie was more timid by far
Than the timidest there.
Once or twice she turned to look
At the bravado-swollen pack.
Slowly the chant began —

'Nellie Mulcahy! Nellie Mulcahy!
Wicked old woman! Wicked old woman!'

One child threw a stone.
Another did likewise.
Soon the little monsters
Were furiously stoning her
Whose name was fear.
When she fell bleeding to the ground,
Whimpering like a beaten pup,
Even then they didn't give up,
But pelted her like mad.

Suddenly they stopped, looked at
Each other, then at Nellie, lying
On the ground, shivering.

Slowly they withdrew
One by one.

Silence. Silence.
All the stones were thrown.

Between the hedges of their guilt
Cain-children shambled home.

Alone,
She dragged herself up,
Crying in small half-uttered moans,
Limped away across the land,
Black bag on her back,
Agony racking her bones.

Between her and the children,
Like hideous forms of fear —
The stones.

Brendan Kennelly

Miller's End

When we moved to Miller's End,
Every afternoon at four
A thin shadow of a shade
Quavered through the garden-door.

Dressed in black from top to toe
And a veil about her head
To us all it seemed as though
She came walking from the dead.

With a basket on her arm
Through the hedge-gap she would pass,
Never a mark that we could spy
On the flagstones or the grass.

When we told the garden-boy
How we saw the phantom glide,
With a grin his face was bright
As the pool he stood beside.

'That's no ghost-walk,' Billy said,
'Nor a ghost you fear to stop —
Only old Miss Wickerby
On a short cut to the shop.'

So next day we lay in wait,
Passed a civil time of day,
Said how pleased we were she came
Daily down our garden-way.

Suddenly her cheek it paled
Turned as quick, from ice to flame.
'Tell me,' said Miss Wickerby.
'Who spoke of me, and my name?'

'Bill the garden-boy.'
She sighed,
Said, 'Of course, you could not know
How he drowned — that very pool —
A frozen winter — long ago.'

Charles Causley

Acrostic

Acrostic means you go a-
Cross the line
Rhyming or
Otherwise, in a
Silly at-
Tempt to
Impress your teacher with a
Clever Poem.

Clive Webster

Cathedral

Come into this quiet place where
Angels carved in stone look down on
Tombs of noble lords and ladies.
Here are stained-glass windows to delight the
Eye and tell us tales of long ago — here the Great West
Door and there an eagle spreads its wings. Here are
Rows and rows of seats and high above each aisle
Arches soar. Come into this quiet place.
Listen to its peace.

June Crebbin

Penguin

Perfectly equipped for swimming, streamlined in
Every detail, see him speed through the water,
Notice how on land, he waddles like an old-fashioned
Gentleman going into dinner,
Up and down he goes, flat-footed, slow. But
In the water he
Never looks absurd, this graceful, polar, water-bird.

June Crebbin

Riddle Poems

1

Riddle my this, riddle my that —
guess my riddle or perhaps not.
What is it you pass going to town
that faces you, and coming from town it
faces you and hasn't moved?

— A tree.

2.

Riddle my this, riddle my that —
guess my riddle or perhaps not.
Boy is sent for something;
something comes back before boy — why?

— Boy climbs tree, picks coconut and drops it.

3.

Riddle my this, riddle my that —
guess my riddle or perhaps not.
Little pools
cluster in my father's yard,
a speck in one and it overflows —
what is it?

— Somebody's eye with dust in it.

4.

Riddle my this, riddle my that —
guess my riddle or perhaps not.
What's hearty as a heart, round as a ring,
dayworker, nightworker, and never eats?

— A pocket watch.

5.

Riddle my this, riddle my that —
guess my riddle, or perhaps not.
What follows king walking, yet stays
watching beggar curled up?

— The moon. Big and bright.

6.

Riddle my this, riddle my that —
guess my riddle, or perhaps not.
Rooms are full, hall is full, but
you can't use a spoonful —
what is it?

— Flames and smoke of a house on fire.

7.

Riddle my this, riddle my that —
guess my riddle, or perhaps not.
Eyes ablaze looking up,
Four-Legs crouch near Four-Legs —
what is it?

— Dog by dinner table. Begging.

8.

Riddle my this, riddle my that —
guess my riddle, or perhaps not.
Waltzing for leaves
waltzing on grass
and put back to stand in corner —
what is it?

— Garden broom that sweeps and is put away.

James Berry

Hatch Me a Riddle

In a little white room
all round and smooth
sits a yellow moon.

In a little white room
once open, for ever open,
sits a yellow moon.

In a little white room,
with neither window nor door,
sits a yellow moon.

Who will break the walls
of the little white room
to steal the yellow moon?

A wise one or a fool?

John Agard

Riddle

For want of a word
the thought was lost;
for want of a thought
the tree was lost;
for want of a tree
the forest was lost;
for want of the forest
a land was lost;
for want of a land
the people were lost;
and all for the want
of one small word ...
   why?

Judith Nicholls

Riddles

We push his nose when we want in
And he must squeal or chime or sing.
Like dentists we say *Open wide!*
And once that's done we slip inside.

Doorbell.

On the top sits fire,
In the middle gold
At the bottom grass.

At the top you stop
In the middle wait
At the bottom, pass.

Traffic lights.

All too liable to snap
And light as a feather,
But willing to stretch the odd point
So when everything is threatening
To fall apart
It holds together.

Rubber band.

Light fingered, invisible
A thief through and through
He'll steal your hat, he'll whip your scarf
And your newspaper too.
He'll hang around street corners
And pounce as you go by
Or hover at your window
And slip in with a sigh.

Wind.

Above the green carpet
The great fried egg
Sits in his blue bath.

Sun in the sky.

George Szirtes

Traditional Riddles in Irish

Bíonn sé laistíos faoi uisce
Bíonn sé lastuas faoi uisce
Agus ní bhuaileann an t-uisce air in aon chor.

Ubh i lacha.

Under the water
Over the water
And never touches the water —
What am I?

An egg inside a duck.

Tá sé an-bhreá
Tá sé buí ina lár,
A sciatháin bán
Agus gan faoi ach aon chos amháin.

Nóinín.

It's very fine
A yellow middle
With white wings
And only one leg.
What's my riddle?

A daisy.

Tá cáilín ar m'aigne agam,
Cáilín beag buí;
Is deas sa lá í,
Is deise san oíche í;
Nuair a ólann sí uisce faigheann sí bás
Ach cuireann an mhóin í ag borradh is ag fás.
Suigh síos ina haice agus má aithníonn tú í,
A chara, céard is ainm do mo cháilín beag buí?

Tine.

I'm thinking of a girl
One yellow and small,
She's pretty by day,
Prettier when night falls;
A drink of water will cause her to die
But turf will nourish and make her grow high.
Sit down beside her and, if you know her at all,
What's the name of my girl yellow and small?

Fire.

translated by
Gabriel Fitzmaurice

Ní Raibh Bríste ar bith ag Brian Ó Loinn

Ní raibh bríste ar bith ag Brian Ó Loinn,
Is cheannaigh sé craiceann seanchaorach ansin;
An olann amuigh is an craiceann istigh
'Sin bríste thar barr!' arsa Brian Ó Loinn.

Traditional

No Trousers at all Had Brian O'Lynn

No trousers at all had Brian O'Lynn
Till he went out and purchased an old sheep's skin,
The wool turned out and the hide turned in —
'That's a fine trousers!' said Brian O'Lynn.

'Ní Raibh Bríste ar bith ag Brian Ó Loinn'
translated from the Irish by Gabriel Fitzmaurice

Hey Diddle Diddle

Hey diddle diddle,
The cat and the fiddle,
The cow jumped over the moon;
the little dog laughed
To see such sport
And the dish ran away with the spoon.

Traditional

Haigh Didil Didil

Haigh didil didil, an cat is an fhidil.
Léim an bhó thar an ré,
An madra beag donn dhein gáire le fonn
Is d'imigh an spúnóg ar strae.

A traditional version in Irish
of 'Hey Diddle Diddle'

Ring-a-Ring o' Roses

Ring-a-ring o' roses,
A pocket full of posies,
A-tishoo! A-tishoo!
We all fall down.

Traditional

Ring-a-Ring-a-Rósaí

Ring-a-ring-a-rósaí
Buidéal lán de *phosies*,
Ceann duitse is ceann domsa.
Is síos linn go léir.

A traditional version in Irish
of Ring-a-Ring o' Roses

Féach

Dreolín
ag tógáil tithe,
a bhean ina
cigire.

Beach
ag filleadh abhaile,
agus í ar
milmheisce.

Coinín
ina sheasamh sa pháirc,
agus é ina
charraig bheo.

Seán Ó hEachtigheirn

Look

A wren
building homes
inspected
by his wife.

A bee
honey-tipsy
returning
to the hive.

A rabbit
standing in a field —
a rock
that's come alive.

*'Féach' translated from the Irish
by Gabriel Fitzmaurice*

Snail

Enjoys the damp. Remembers smell of sea.
Once moved with fish, swaying anemone,
the steady knock and whisper of the swell.
Coiled now in dead and mottled shell,
boneless and moist, peering with pimple-eyes,
creature of chilly dawn, the soft moonrise.
And with what slow and persevering toil
he plots his route along the easy soil,
sampling each tangled leaf and dewy stem,
writing in slimy signs his requiem,
until when summer's burning finger warns,
he probes the air with dry and anxious horns,
and then his final exploration past,
discards his china house and home at last.

Leonard Clark

Small, Smaller

I thought that I knew all there was to know
Of being small, until I saw once, black against the snow,
A shrew, trapped in my footprint, jump and fall
And jump again and fall, the hole too deep, the walls too tall.

Russell Hoban

I Saw a Jolly Hunter

I saw a jolly hunter
With a jolly gun
Walking in the country
In the jolly sun.

In the jolly meadow
Sat a jolly hare.
Saw the jolly hunter.
Took jolly care.

Hunter jolly eager —
Sight of jolly prey.
Forgot gun pointing
Wrong jolly way.

Jolly hunter jolly head
Over heels gone.
Jolly old safety-catch
Not jolly on.

Bang went the jolly gun.
Hunter jolly dead.
Jolly hare got clean away.
Jolly good, I said.

Charles Causley

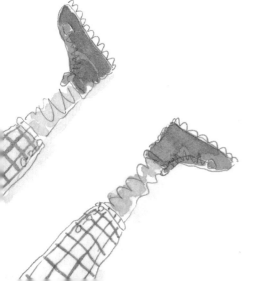

Charlotte's Dog

Daniel the spaniel has ears like rugs,
Teeth like prongs of electric plugs.

His back's a thundery winter sky,
Black clouds, white clouds rumbling by.

His nose is the rubber of an old squash ball
Bounced in the rain. His tail you'd call

A chopped-off rope with a motor inside
That keeps it walloping. Red-rimmed-eyed,

He whimpers like plimsolls on a wooden floor.
When he yawns he closes a crimson door.

When he barks it's a shark of a sound that bites
Through frosty mornings and icy nights.

When he sleeps he wheezes on a dozing lung:
Then he wakes you too with a wash of his tongue!

Kit Wright

An Breac

'Tá spotaí os comhair mo shúl,' arsan breac.
'Maith thú!' arsan bradán.

Is má chreideann tú an scéal sin
Níl ionat ach amadán!

Gabriel Rosenstock

The Trout

'There are spots before my eyes,' says the trout.
The salmon says, 'That's cool!'

(And if you believe this rubbish
You're nothing but a fool!)

'An Breac' translated from the Irish
by Gabriel Fitzmaurice

Snáthaid an Phúca

'Tá pianta im chosa,'
Dúirt snáthaid an phúca.
Tháinig an dochtúir
'Seo dhá chiúibín siúcra;
Leigheasfaidh sé sin thú,
Ní bhfaighidh tú bás,
Níl rud ar bith cearr leat —
Ach go bhfuil rú ag fás!'

Gabriel Rosenstock

Daddy-Long-Legs

'I've a pain in my legs,'
The Daddy-long-legs cried;
'Take two sugar-lumps,'
The doctor replied;
'That will surely cure you,
You're not going to die;
There's nothing the matter —
You're growing up, my boy!'

'Snáthaid an Phúca' translated from the Irish
by Gabriel Fitzmaurice

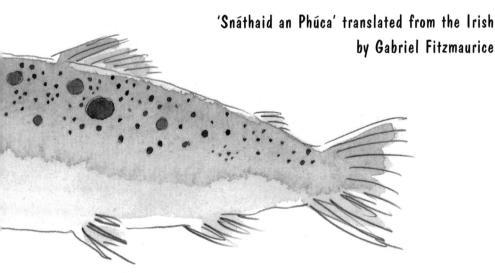

91

Malairt

'Gaibh i leith,' arsa Turnbull, 'go bhfeice tú an brón
 I súilibh an chapaill,
Dá mbeadh crúba chomh mór leo sin fútsa bheadh brón
Id shúilibh chomh maith leis.'

Agus b'fhollas gur thuig sé chomh maith sin an brón
I súilibh an chapaill,
Is gur mhachnaigh chomh cruaidh sin gur tomadh
 é fá dheoidh
In aigne an chapaill.

D'fhéachas ar an gcapall go bhfeicinn an brón
'Na shúilibh ag seasamh,
Do chonac súile Turnbull ag féachaint im threo
As cloigeann an chapaill.

D'fhéachas ar Turnbull is d'fhéachas air fá dhó
Is do chonac ar a leacain
Na súile rómhóra a bhí balbh le brón —
Súile an chapaill.

Seán Ó Ríordáin

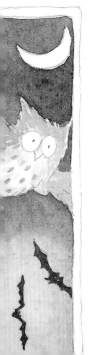

A Change

'Come over,' said Turnbull, 'and look at the sorrow
In the horse's eyes.
If you had hooves under you like those
There would be sorrow in your eyes.'

And 'twas plain that he knew this sorrow so well
In the horse's eyes
And he wondered so deeply that he dived in the end
Into the horse's mind.

I looked at the horse then that I might see
The sorrow in his eyes
And Turnbull's eyes were looking at me
From the horse's mind.

I looked at Turnbull and looked once again
And there in Turnbull's head —
Not Turnbull's eyes, but, dumb with grief
Were the horse's eyes instead.

'Malairt' translated from the Irish
by Gabriel Fitzmaurice

The Bat

By day the bat is cousin to the mouse.
He likes the attic of an ageing house.

His fingers make a hat about his head.
His pulse is so slow we think him dead.

He loops in crazy figures half the night
Among the trees that face the corner light.

But when he brushes up against a screen,
We are afraid of what our eyes have seen:

For something is amiss or out of place
When mice with wings can wear a human face.

Theodore Roethke

The Blackbird
by Belfast Lough

What little throat
Has framed that note?
What gold beak shot
It far away?
A blackbird on
His leafy throne
Tossed it all alone
Across the bay.

*Anon: Translated from the Irish
by Frank O'Connor*

A Bird Came Down the Walk

A Bird came down the Walk —
He did not know I saw —
He bit an Angleworm in halves
And ate the fellow, raw,

And then he drank a Dew
From a convenient Grass —
And then hopped sidewise to the Wall
To let a Beetle pass —

He glanced with rapid eyes
That hurried all around —
They looked like frightened Beads, I thought —
He stirred his Velvet Head

Like one in danger, Cautious;
I offered him a Crumb
And he unrolled his feathers
And rowed him softer home —

Than Oars divide the Ocean,
Too silver for a seam —
Or Butterflies, off Bank of Noon
Leap, plashless as they swim.

Emily Dickinson

The Owl and the Pussy-Cat

The Owl and the Pussy-Cat went to sea
In a beautiful pea-green boat:
They took some honey, and plenty of money
Wrapped up in a five-pound note.
The Owl looked up to the stars above,
And sang to a small guitar,
'O lovely Pussy, O Pussy, my love,
What a beautiful Pussy you are,
You are,
You are!
What a beautiful Pussy you are!'

Pussy said to the Owl, 'You elegant fowl,
How charmingly sweet you sing!
Oh! let us be married; too long we have tarried
But what shall we do for a ring?'
They sailed away, for a year and a day,
To the land where the bong-tree grows;
And there in a wood a Piggy-wig stood,
With a ring at the end of his nose,
His nose,
His nose,
With a ring at the end of his nose.

'Dear Pig, are you willing to sell for one shilling
Your ring?' Said the Piggy, 'I will.'
So they took it away, and were married next day
By the turkey who lives on the hill.
They dined on mince and slices of quince,
Which they ate with a runcible spoon;
And hand in hand, on the edge of the sand,
They danced by the light of the moon,
The moon,
The moon,
They danced by the light of the moon.

Edward Lear

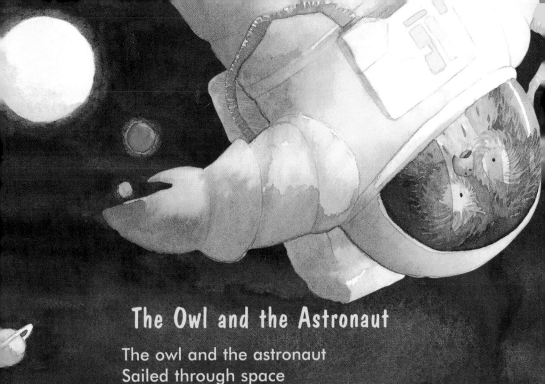

The Owl and the Astronaut

The owl and the astronaut
Sailed through space
In their intergalactic ship
They kept hunger at bay
With three pills a day
And drank through a protein drip.
The owl dreamed of mince
And slices of quince
And remarked how life had gone flat;
'It may be all right
To fly faster than light
But I preferred the boat and the cat.'

Gareth Owen

Pangur Bán

Written by a student of the monastery of Carinthia on a copy of St Paul's Epistles, in the eighth century

I and Pangur Bán, my cat,
'Tis like task we are at;
Hunting mice is his delight
Hunting words I sit all night.

Better far than praise of men
'Tis to sit with book and pen;
Pangur bears me no ill-will,
He too plies his simple skill.

'Tis a merry thing to see
At our tasks how glad are we,
When at home we sit and find
Entertainment to our mind.

Oftentimes a mouse will stray
In the hero Pangur's way;
Oftentimes my keen thought set
Takes a meaning in its net.

'Gainst the wall he sets his eye
Full and fierce and sharp and sly;
'Gainst the wall of knowledge I
All my little wisdom try.

When a mouse darts from its den,
O how glad is Pangur then!
O what gladness do I prove
When I solve the doubts I love!

So in peace our tasks we ply,
Pangur Bán, my cat, and I;
In our arts we find our bliss,
I have mine and he has his.

Practice every day has made
Pangur perfect in his trade;
I get wisdom day and night
Turning darkness into light.

Anon

Translated from the Irish by Robin Flower

The Tyger

Tyger! Tyger! burning bright
In the forests of the night,
What immortal hand or eye
Could frame thy fearful symmetry?

In what distant deeps or skies
Burnt the fire of thine eyes?
On what wings dare he aspire?
What the hand dare seize the fire?

And what shoulder, & what art,
Could twist the sinews of thy heart?
And when thy heart began to beat,
What dread hand? & what dread feet?

What the hammer? What the chain?
In what furnace was thy brain?
What the anvil? What dead grasp
Dare its deadly terrors clasp?

When the stars threw down their spear
And water'd Heaven with their tears,
Did he smile his work to see?
Did he who made the Lamb make thee?

Tyger! Tyger! burning bright
In the forests of the night,
What immortal hand or eye
Dare frame thy fearful symmetry?

William Blake

Tiger

Tiger, eyes dark with
half-remembered forest night,
stalks an empty cage.

Judith Nicholls

101

The Woodland Haiku

Fox

Slinks to the wood's edge
and — with one paw raised — surveys
the open meadows.

Rabbits

Blind panic sets in
and they're off, like dodgem cars
gone out of control.

Owl

Blip on his radar
sends owl whooshing through the dark,
homing in on rats, mice.

Sheep's skull

Whitened and toothless
discovered in a damp ditch.
A trophy for home.

Fallow deer

Moving smooth as smoke
she starts at an air tremor.
Is gone like a ghost.

Rooks

They float high above,
black as scraps of charred paper
drifting from a fire.

Pike

Killer submarine
he lurks deep in the woodland's
green-skinned pond. Lurks .... strikes.

Humans

Clumsy, twig-snapping,
they see nothing but trees, trees.
The creatures hide ... watch....

Wes Magee

An Mhuc

'Tá tinneas fiacaile i mo chluas, an bhféadfá mé a leigheas?'
'Cinnte,' arsa an dochtúir is thóg sé anuas an deimheas.
Thosnaigh an mhuc ag scréachaíl; arsa an dochtúir. 'Cad tá cearr?'
'Dada, a dhochtúir, dada! Tá mé míle uair níos fearr!'

Gabriel Rosenstock

The Pig

'Doctor can you cure me? I've a toothache in my ears.'
'Sure,' says the doctor taking down a shears.
'What's up?' says the doctor, 'why're you squealing, sow?'
'Nothing, doctor, nothing, I'm much better now.'

'An Mhuc' translated from the Irish
by Gabriel Fitzmaurice

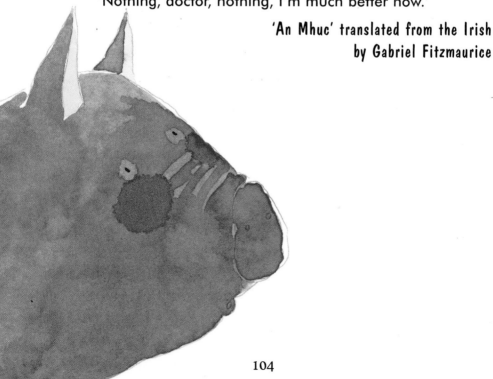

104

The Horse

The horse moves
independently
without reference
to his load

He has eyes
like a woman and
turns them
about, throws

back his ears
and is generally
conscious of
the world. Yet

he pulls when
he must and
pulls well, blowing
fog from

his nostrils
like fumes from
the twin
exhausts of a car.

William Carlos Williams

Teilifís

(faoi m'iníon Saffron)

Ar a cúig a chlog ar maidin
Theastaigh an teilifís uaithi.
An féidir argóint le beainín
Dhá bhliain go leith?
Síos linn le chéile
Níor bhacas fiú le gléasadh
Is bhí an seomra préachta.
Gan solas fós sa spéir
Stánamar le hiontas ar scáileán bán.
Anois! Sásta?
Ach chonaic sise sneachta
Is sioraf tríd an sneachta
Is ulchabhán Artach
Ag faoileáil
Os a chionn.

Gabriel Rosenstock

Television

(for my daughter Saffron)

At five o'clock in the morning
She wanted television.
Who can argue with a little woman
Two and a half years old?
Down we went together
I didn't even dress
And the room was freezing.
No light yet in the sky
We stared in wonder at the white screen.
Happy now?
But she saw snow
And a giraffe through it
And an arctic owl
Wheeling
Above it.

'Teilifís' translated from the Irish
by Gabriel Fitzmaurice

Poem from a Three-Year-Old

And will the flowers die?

And will the people die?

And every day do you grow old, do I
grow old, no I'm not old, do
flowers grow old?

Old things — do you throw them out?

Do you throw old people out?

And how you know a flower that's old?

The petals fall, the petals fall from flowers,
and do the petals fall from people too,
every day more petals fall until the
floor where I would like to play I
want to play is covered with old
flowers and people all the same
together lying there with petals fallen
on the dirty floor I want to play
the floor you come and sweep
with the huge broom.

The dirt you sweep, what happens that,
what happens all the dirt you sweep
from flowers and people, what
happens all the dirt? Is all the
dirt what's left of flowers and
people, all the dirt there in a
heap under the huge broom that
sweeps everything away?

Why you work so hard, why brush
and sweep to make a heap of dirt?
And who will bring new flowers?
And who will bring new people? Who will
bring new flowers to put in water
where no petals fall on to the
floor where I would like to
play? Who will bring new flowers
that will not hang their heads
like tired old people wanting sleep?
Who will bring new flowers that
do not split and shrivel every
day? And if we have new flowers,
will we have new people too to
keep the flowers alive and give
them water?

And will the new young flowers die?

And will the new young people die?

And why?

Brendan Kennelly

Night Feed

This is dawn.
Believe me
This is your season, little daughter.
The moment daisies open,
The hour mercurial rainwater
Makes a mirror for sparrows.
It's time we drowned our sorrows.

I tiptoe in.
I lift you up
Wriggling
In your rosy, zipped sleeper.
Yes, this is the hour
For the early bird and me
When finder is keeper.

I crook the bottle.
How you suckle!
This is the best I can be,
Housewife
To this nursery
Where you hold on,
Dear life.

A silt of milk
The last suck.
And now your eyes are open,
Birth-coloured and offended.
Earth wakes.
You go back to sleep.
The feed is ended.

Worms turn.
Stars go in.
Even the moon is losing face.
Poplars stilt for dawn
And we begin
The long fall from grace
I tuck you in.

Eavan Boland

Whose Baby?

The spoon misses her mouth
She bangs it on the table in frustration.
She likes to feed herself
And cries if I help her.

I bring her a mirror
I wipe the food off her face.
She watches her life
Going backwards.

She can't walk or crawl
But has already passed her exams,
Been married and read more books
Than I ever could.

Now I read to her at night
And I struggle with words
Which are easy for her mind
But impossible on her lips.

'Good night, Mum,' I whisper.
The crooked smile she returns
Is not at all like a baby's
Though it still says everything she can't.

Lindsay MacRae

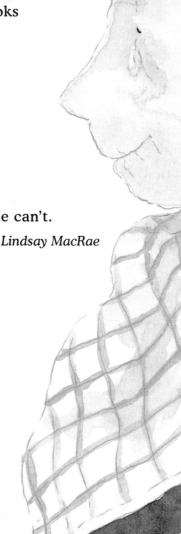

Good Night

Will you leave the light, Tom? Just a while.
You've already discovered what night means
Now that the bars have come down from your cot;
Nothing to protect you but the brittle
Cobwebby veil of sleep. Four a.m. scenes
And repeated stories are all we've got
To send you back to the enveloping peace.
And where does it come from, this new disease
Of darkness, the fear of the night's unseen?
How many deaths have you witnessed on the small screen
Already, murders while nappy-changing,
Shooting between bottles and Sudocrem?
No Care Bears can protect your naked toes,
No Megan watch the sky while you doze.

Thomas McCarthy

Dream and Forgetting

My little girl is afraid to go to sleep.
Repeatedly she'll call me to her bed.
Perspiring gently when her slumber's deep
She trembles when I go to stroke her head.
She wakes so easily. Her eyes flick open,
She sits straight up, asks for a drink but can't
Get back to where she was. She can be woken
By a creaking floorboard. We know she wants
To only be with us, where we are, here.
She knows the hiding place we can't discover
And also what it is she cannot near.
She says goodnight as if it were for ever.
I sit in darkness, hear her breathing pulse
And slowly find I'm here and there at once.

Gyözö Ferencz
Translated by George Szirtes

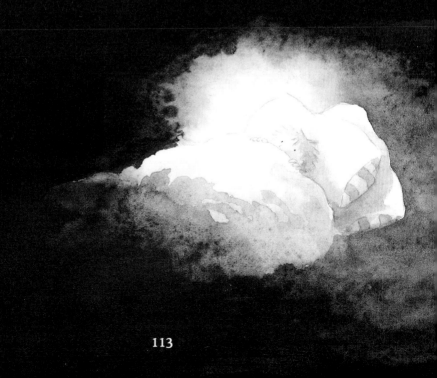

Growing Pain

The boy was barely five years old.
We sent him to the little school
And left him there to learn the names
Of flowers in jam jars on the sill
And learn to do as he was told.
He seemed quite happy there until
Three weeks afterwards, at night,
The darkness whimpered in his room.
I went upstairs, switched on his light,
And found him wide awake, distraught,
Sheets mangled and his eiderdown
Untidy carpet on the floor.
I said, 'Why can't you sleep? A pain?'
He snuffled, gave a little moan,
And then he spoke a single word:
'Jessica.' The sound was blurred.
'Jessica? What do you mean?'
'A girl at school called Jessica,
She hurts —' he touched himself between
The heart and stomach '— she has been
Aching here and I can see her.'
Nothing I had read or heard
Instructed me in what to do.
I covered him and stroked his head.
'The pain will go, in time,' I said.

Vernon Scannel

When All the Others

When all the others were away at Mass
I was all hers as we peeled potatoes.
They broke the silence, let fall one by one
Like solder weeping off the soldering iron:
Cold comforts set between us, things to share
Gleaming in a bucket of clean water.
And again let fall. Little pleasant splashes
From each other's work would bring us to our senses.

So while the parish priest at her bedside
Went hammer and tongs at the prayers for the dying
And some were responding and some crying
I remembered her head bent towards my head,
Her breath in mine, our fluent dipping knives —
Never closer the whole rest of our lives.

Seamus Heaney

A Small Girl Swinging

When first they pushed me
I was very scared.
My tummy jiggled. I was
Unprepared.

The second time was higher
And my ears
Were cold with whisperings
Of tiny fears.

The third time up was HIGH,
My teeth on edge.
My heart leapt off the bedroom
Windowledge.

The fourth time, Oh, the fourth time
It was mad.
My skirt flew off the world
And I was glad.

No one's pushing now,
My ears are ringing.
Who'll see across the park
A small girl swinging?

Who'll hear across the park
Her mother calling,
And everywhere her shadows
Rising, falling?

George Szirtes

The Land of Counterpane

When I was sick and lay a-bed,
I had two pillows at my head,
And all my toys beside me lay
To keep me happy all the day.

And sometimes for an hour or so
I watched my leaden soldiers go,
With different uniforms and drills,
Among the bed-clothes, through the hills;

And sometimes sent my ships in fleets
All up and down among the sheets;
Or brought my trees and houses out,
And planted cities all about.

I was the giant great and still
That sits upon the pillow hill,
And sees before him, dale and plain,
The pleasant land of counterpane.

Robert Louis Stevenson

Sickroom

Regularly I visited,
since your sickness,
you in the black bedroom
with the gauze of death
around you like your sheets.

Now I must be frank:
these are not roses beside you,
nor are these grapes,
and this is no portrait
of your father's friend.

I know you cannot rise.
You are unable to move.
But I can see your fear,
for two wet mice
dart
cornered in the hollows
of your head.

Michael Hartnett

Grandad

Grandad's dead
And I'm sorry about that.

He'd a huge black overcoat
He felt proud in it.
You could have hidden
A football crowd in it.
Far too big —
It was a lousy fit
But Grandad didn't
Mind a bit.
He wore it all winter
With a squashed black hat.

Now he's dead
And I'm sorry about that.

He'd got twelve stories.
I'd heard every one of them
Hundreds of times
But that was the fun of them:
You knew what was coming
So you could join in.
He'd got big hands
And brown, grooved skin
And when he laughed
It knocked you flat.

Now he's dead
And I'm sorry about that.

Kit Wright

Until Gran Died

The minnows I caught
lived for a few days in a jar
then floated side-up on the surface.
We buried them beneath the hedge.
I didn't cry, but felt sad inside.

I thought
I could deal with funerals,
that is until Gran died.

The goldfish I kept in a bowl
passed away with old age.
Mum wrapped him in newspaper
and we buried him next to a rose bush.
I didn't cry, but felt sad inside.

I thought
I could deal with funerals
that is until Gran died.

My cat lay stiff in a shoe box
after being hit by a car.
Dad dug a hole and we buried her
under the apple tree.
I didn't cry, but felt very sad inside.

I thought
I could deal with funerals,
that is until Gran died.

And when she died
I went to the funeral
with relations dressed in black.
They cried, and so did I.
Salty tears ran down my face.
Oh, how I cried.

Yes, I thought
I could deal with funerals,
that is until Gran died.

She was buried in a graveyard
and even the sky wept that day
Rain fell and fell and fell,
and thunder sobbed far away
across the town,
I cried and I cried.

I thought
I could deal with funerals,
that is until Gran
died.

Wes Magee

Dínit An Bhróin

Nochtaíodh domsa tráth
Dínit mhór an bhróin,
Ar fheiceáil dom beirt bhan
Ag siúl amach ó shlua
I bhfeisteas caointe dubh
Gan focal astu beirt:
D'imigh an dínit leo
Ón slua callánach mór.

Bhí freastalán istigh
Ó línéar ar an ród,
Fuadar faoi gach n-aon,
Gleo ann is caint ard;
Ach an bheirt a bhí ina dtost,
A shiúil amach leo féin
I bhfeisteas caointe dubh,
D'imigh an dínit leo.

Máirtín Ó Direáin

The Dignity of Grief

Grief's great dignity
Was revealed to me once,
On seeing two women
Emerging from a crowd
In black mourning
Each without a word:
Dignity left with them
From the large and clamorous throng.

A tender was in
From a liner in the roads,
And everyone was rushing,
There was tumult and loud talk;
But the pair who were silent
Who walked out on their own
In black mourning
Left with dignity.

*'Dínit An Bhróin' translated from the Irish
by Gabriel Fitzmaurice*

All of Us

All of us are afraid
More often than we tell.

There are times we cling like mussels to the sea-wall,
And pray that the pounding waves
Won't smash our shell.

Times we hear nothing but the sound
Of our loneliness, like a cracked bell
From fields far away where the trees are in icy shade.

O many a time in the night-time and in the day,
More often than we say,
We are afraid.

If people say they are never frightened,
I don't believe them.
If people say they are frightened,
I want to retrieve them

From that dark shivering haunt
Where they don't want to be,
Nor I.

Let's make of ourselves, therefore, an enormous sky
Over whatever
We must hold dear.

And we'll comfort each other,
Comfort each other's
Fear.

Kit Wright

Goodbye

I'm running away, you can't stop me.
I've put what I need in my bag.
I've my blue hippopotamus, big painted pebble,
And yellow pyjamas with stripes that zigzag.

You shouted at me so I'm going.
You'll be sorry when I've gone away.
You'll say, 'How I wish I'd been nicer to her!'
But it's no good, I've packed, I'm not going to stay.

I'm opening the door, yes I mean it,
So quick, you'd better be nice.
When I'm gone you'll have no one to make bubble baths for
Or chocolate cakes or marzipan mice.

I expect you'll be lonely without me,
You'll have no one to read comics to,
So I'm going to give you your very last chance,
Though you're mean I've decided to stay here with you.

Michelle Magorian

One

Only one of me
and nobody can get a second one
from a photocopy machine.

Nobody has the fingerprints I have.
Nobody can cry my tears, or laugh my laugh
or have my expectancy when I wait.

But anybody can mimic my dance with my dog.
Anybody can howl how I sing out of tune.
And mirrors can show me multiplied
many times, say, dressed up in red
or dressed up in grey.

Nobody can get into my clothes for me
or feel my fall for me, or do my running.
Nobody hears my music for me, either.

I am just this one.
Nobody else makes the words
I shape with sound, when I talk.

But anybody can act how I stutter in a rage.
Anybody can copy echoes I make.
And mirrors can show me multiplied
many times, say, dressed up in green
or dressed up in blue.

James Berry

Computer Games

Computer games
Are the thing to play
On another boring day —
Chasing sonic,
Tagging tails
Passes time,
Never fails;

But what if, one day,
All we do
Is play computers
Through and through
From day's first light
To day's dark end
And never again play
'Let's Pretend'?

Lee Dellow

127

Into the Unknown

Like a bird
that has flown
Like a tree
that has grown

Like a cathedral
rising from
a prison of stone
Like a soul
flying from
a house of bone

I will leap
into the unknown

Calling my life my own

John Agard

Wee Hughie

He's gone to school, Wee Hughie,
An' him not four,
Sure I saw the fright was in him
When he left the door.

But he took a hand of Denny
An' a hand of Dan,
Wi' Joe's owld coat upon him —
Och, the poor wee man!

He cut the quarest figure,
More stout nor thin,
An' trottin' right an' steady,
Wi' his toes turned in.

I watched him to the corner
O' the big turf stack,
An' the more his feet went forrit,
Still his head turned back.

He was lookin', would I call him,
Och, me heart was woe —
Sure it's lost I am without him,
But he be to go.

I followed to the turnin'
When he passed it by,
God help him, he was cryin'
And maybe so was I.

Elizabeth Shane

Blue Umbrellas

'The thing that makes a blue umbrella with its tail —
How do you call it?' you ask. Poorly and pale
Comes my answer. For all I can call it is peacock.

Now that you go to school, you will learn how we call
    all sorts of things;
How we mar great works by our mean recital.
You will learn, for instance, that Head Monster
    is not the gentleman's accepted title;
The blue-tailed eccentrics will be merely peacocks;
    the dead bird will no longer doze
Off till tomorrow's lark, for the letter has killed him.
The dictionary is opening, the gay umbrellas close.

Oh our mistaken teachers! —
It was not a proper respect for words that we need,
But a decent regard for things, those older creatures
    and more real.
Later you may even resort to writing verse
To prove the dishonesty of names and their black greed —
To confess your ignorance, to expiate your crime,
    seeking a spell to lift a curse.
Or you may, more commodiously, spy on your children,
    busy discoverers,
Without the dubious benefit of rhyme.

D.J. Enright

Colour of My Dreams

I'm a really rotten reader
the worst in all the class,
the sort of rotten reader
that makes you want to laugh.

I'm last in all the readin' tests,
my score's not on the page
and when I read to teacher
she gets in such a rage.

She says I cannot form my words
she says I can't build up
and that I don't know phonics
— and don't know c-a-t from k-u-p.

They say that I'm dyxlectic
(that's a word they've just found out)
... but when I get some plasticine
I know what that's about.

I make these scary monsters
I draw these secret lands
and get my hair all sticky
and paint on all me hands.

I make these super models,
I build these smashing towers
that reach up to the ceiling
— and take me hours and hours.

I paint these lovely pictures
in thick green drippy paint
that gets all on the carpet —
and makes the cleaners faint.

I build great magic forests
weave bushes out of string
and paint pink panderellos
and birds that really sing.

I play my world of real believe
I play it every day
and teachers stand and watch me
but don't know what to say.

They give me diagnostic tests,
they try out reading schemes,
but none of them will ever know
the colour of my dreams.

Peter Dixon

What Happens to the Colors?

What happens to the colors
when night replaces day?
What turns the wrens to ravens,
the trees to shades of gray?

Who paints away the garden
when the sky's a sea of ink?
Who robs the sleeping flowers
of their purple and their pink?

What makes the midnight clover
quiver black upon the lawn?
What happens to the colors?
What brings them back at dawn?

Jack Prelutsky

I Asked the Little Boy who Cannot See

I asked the little boy who cannot see,
'And what is colour like?'
'Why, green,' said he,
'Is like the rustle when the wind blows through
The forest; running water, that is blue;
And red is like a trumpet sound; and pink
Is like the smell of roses; and I think
That purple must be like a thunderstorm;
And yellow is like something soft and warm;
And white is a pleasant stillness when you lie
and dream.'

Anon

Streemin

im in the botom streme
wich means im not britgh

dont lik readin
cant hardly write

But all these divishns
arnt reelly fair

Look at the cemtery
no streemin there

Roger McGough

Slow Reader

He can make sculptures
and fabulous machines,
invent games, tell jokes,
give solemn, adult advice —
but he is slow to read.
When I take him on my knee
with his Ladybird book
he gazes into the air,
sighing and shaking his head
like an old man
who knows the mountains
are impassable.

He toys with words,
letting them go cold
as gristly meat,
until I relent
and let him wiggle free:
a fish returning
to its element,
or a white-eyed colt — shying
from the bit — who sees
that if he takes it
in his mouth
he'll never run
quite free again.

Vicki Feaver

The Ghost Teacher

The school is closed, the children gone,
But the ghost of a teacher lingers on.
As the daylight fades, as the daytime ends,
As the night draws in and the dark descends,
She stands in the classroom, as clear as glass,
And calls the names of her absent class.

The school is shut, the children grown,
But the ghost of the teacher, all alone,
Puts the date on the board and moves about
(As the night draws on and the stars come out)
Between the desks — a glow in the gloom —
And calls for quiet in the silent room.

The school is a ruin, the children fled,
But the ghost of the teacher, long-time dead,
As the moon comes up and the first owls glide,
Puts on her coat and steps outside.
In the moonlit playground, shadow-free
She stands on duty with a cup of tea.

The school is forgotten — children forget —
But the ghost of a teacher lingers yet.
As the night creeps up to the edge of the day,
She tidies the Plasticine away;
Counts the scissors — a shimmer of glass —
And says, 'Off you go!' to her absent class

She utters the words that no one hears,
Picks up her bag ...

    and
    disappears.

Allan Ahlberg

The Lesson

'Blether, blather, blah-blah, bosh.
Claptrap, humbug, poppycock, tosh.
Guff, flap-doodle, gas and gabble.
Hocus pocus, gibberish, babble.
Baloney, hooey, jabber, phew,
Stuff and nonsense, drivel, moo.
Rhubarb, rhubarb, rhubarb, banter.
Prattle, waffle, rave and ranter.
Rubbish, piffle, tommy-rot, guff,
Twaddle, bilge, bombast, bluff.
Thank you.'

Colin McNaughton

Nobody

I'm Nobody! Who are you?
Are you — Nobody — too?
Then there's a pair of us!
Don't tell! they'd banish us — you know!

How dreary — to be — Somebody!
How public — like a Frog —
To tell your name — the livelong June —
To an admiring Bog!

Emily Dickinson

A Boy

Half a mile from the sea,
in a house with a dozen bedrooms
he grew up. Who was he?
Oh, nobody much. A boy
with the usual likes
and more than a few dislikes.
Did he swim much? Nah,
that sea was the Atlantic
and out there is Iceland.
He kept his play inland
on an L-shaped football pitch
between the garage and the gate.
What did he eat?
Stuff his grandfather made,
home-made sausages,
potted pig's head.
He got the library keys
and carried eight books at a time
home, and he read.
He read so much
he stayed in the book's world.
Wind rattled the window
of his third-storey room,
but his bed was warm.
And he stayed in his bed
half the day if he could,
reading by candlelight
when the storms struck
and the electricity died.
How do I know all this?
You'd guess how if you tried.

Matthew Sweeney

Happy Birthday from Bennigans

Why did you do it, Mother?
I told you — didn't I — that I'd go with you
to a restaurant for my birthday
on one condition: Don't go and blab
to the waitress it's my BIG DAY.
But you had to go and tell her.
God, what if somebody had seen me?
I realize that you and Daddy
simply do not care if you ruin my reputation.
I almost thought for a teensy second
you had restrained yourself for once.
But no. You and your big mouth.
'Hip, hop, happy, b, birth, day,
hap, hap, happy, Happy Birthday to You!':
a zero girl, singing a zero song
at the top of her nothingness of a voice.
'All of us at Bennigans hope it's a special day!'
All of them, Mother, not just some.
That's IT for birthdays from now on.
Next year I'll be celebrating by myself.

Julie O'Callaghan

Skilly Oogan

Skilly Oogan's no one you can see,
And no one else can be his friend but me.
Skilly lives where swallows live, away up high
Beneath the topmost eaves against the sky.
When all the world's asleep on moonlit nights,
Up on our roof he flies his cobweb kites.
He has an acorn boat that, when it rains,
He sails in gutters, even down the drains.
Sometimes he hides in letters that I write —
Snug in the envelope and out of sight,
On six-cent stamps he travels in all weathers
And with the midnight owl returns on silent feathers.
In summer time he rides the dragonflies
Above the pond, and looks in bullfrogs' eyes
For his reflection when he combs his hair.
And sometimes when I want him he's not there;
But mostly Skilly Oogan's where I think he'll be,
And no one even knows his name but me.

Russell Hoban

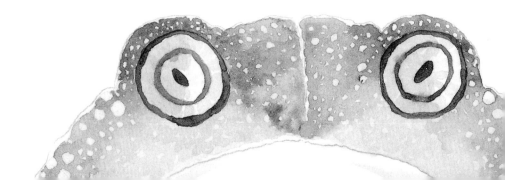

Why Brownlee Left

Why Brownlee left, and where he went,
Is a mystery even now.
For if a man should have been content
It was him; two acres of barley,
One of potatoes, four bullocks,
A milker, a slated farmhouse.
He was last seen going out to plough
On a March morning, bright and early.

By noon Brownlee was famous;
They had found all abandoned, with
The last rig unbroken, his pair of black
Horses, like man and wife,
Shifting their weight from foot to
Foot, and gazing into the future.

Paul Muldoon

Scarecrow

the scarecrow
looks sad tonight all covered in rags
her solitude made of sticks
flapping in the dark field
and her eyes that won't shut
watching the cows at sleep.
with no shoes
and wind in her pockets,
she counts those stars
she can see
from her fixed angle
and listens to the black sticks rubbing
as she spits her curses at the moon.

Stef Pixner

rain or hail

rain or hail
sam done
the best he kin
till they digged his hole

:sam was a man

stout as a bridge
rugged as a bear
slickern a weazel
how be you

(sun or snow)

gone into what
like all them kings
you read about
and on him sings

a whippoorwill;

heart was big
as the world aint square
with room for the devil
and his angels too

yes, sir

what may be better
or what may be worse
and what may be clover
clover clover

(nobody'll know)

sam was a man
grinned his grin
done his chores
laid him down.

Sleep well

E. E. Cummings

Beebla

for John and Nessa

Beebla wasn't sure that he was born
(What was it to be born? He didn't know),
But his mother had been dying four or five times:
Beebla threatened God: 'Don't let her go —
If You do, then I won't say my prayers;
If You do, then I won't go to Mass.'
The priest came and anointed Beebla's Mammy.
Next morning, Beebla boasted in his class:
'My mother was anointed in the night-time;
The priest came to our house, I stayed up late.'
Beebla was cock-proud of his achievement:
All the class was listening — this was great!

Beebla played with all the boys at playtime
(The girls were in the school across the way) —
They played football with a sock stuffed with old papers,
He'd forget about his Mammy in the play.
But always at the back of all his playing,
He knew about anointing in the night,
And, knowing this, there could be no un-knowing —
Nothing in the world, would change that quite.

Beebla got a motor-car in London —
A blue one with pedals which he craved
(Beebla'd been in hospital in London,
And, coming home, he'd had to have his way);
So his Daddy bought him his blue motor-car,
He drove it all the way out to the 'plane,
And touching down, cranky with excitement,
He squealed till he was in his car again.

He drove around the village, a born show-off;
He pulled into a funeral, kept his place,
And all the funeral cars, backed up behind him,
Couldn't hoot, for that would be disgrace!

He drove off from the Chapel to the graveyard,
And, tiring, he pulled out and headed back;
When his mother heard about it, she went purple
And grabbed for her *wallop-spoon* to smack;
But his Daddy shielded Beebla from her wallops —
They brushed across his Daddy's legs until
His mother's rage fizzled to a token:
She shook the spoon, and threatened that she'd kill
Him if he didn't mind his manners;
But Beebla went on driving, till one day
A real car almost hit him at the Corner
For safety, they took his car away.
Beebla didn't cry or throw a tantrum —
He knew that but for luck he would be dead,
And at night-time, after kisses, hugs and lights-out,
He started up his car inside his head.

Beebla got a piano once from Santa —
He ran down to the Church on Christmas Day
Before his Mammy or his Daddy could contain him
(He wanted all the crowd to hear him play).
And he walloped notes and pounded them and thumped them
As *Silent Night* became a noisy day,
But it was his noise, all his own and he could make it —
It said things for him that only it could say.

And he stole into the Church another morning
When all the crowd had scattered home from Mass,
And he went up to the *mike* like Elvis Presley
But he only made an echo — it was off!
So Beebla went back home to his piano,
To the sound of what it is to be alone
Cos Beebla had no brothers or no sisters
And he often had to play all on his own.

Beebla was the crossest in the village —
He was not afraid of beast or man:
He'd jump off walls, climb trees, walk under horses —

He did it for a dare; until the Wren
When the Wren Boys dressed up in masks and sashes
And came into your house to dance and play —
Beebla was excited at the Wren Boys,
He simply couldn't wait for Stephen's Day;
But when the Wren Boys came to Beebla's kitchen
Like horrors that he dreaded in his dreams,
He howled, tore off into the bathroom,
And hid behind the bath and kicked and screamed.
His mother came and told him not to worry,
Brought Tom Mangan into him without the mask —
Tom Mangan was his friend, worked in the Creamery,
But today Tom Mangan caused his little heart
To pound inside his ribcage like a nightmare,
Was fear dressed up and playing for hard cash —
Tom would be his friend again tomorow,
But today Beebla hung around the bath.

He ran away from school the day he started —
He ran before he got inside the door
And his friends who'd brought him there that morning
Couldn't catch him. But he'd no time to explore
The village that morning in December
Before Christmas trees were common, or lights lit —
Beebla had to figure out his problem
And he wasn't sure how he'd get out of it.

He stole into his shop and no one noticed
(His Daddy's shop, his Mammy wasn't well)
And he hid beneath the counter till Daddy found him:
'Oh Daddy, Daddy, Daddy, please don't tell
Mammy that I ran from school this morning —
The doors were big and dark, the windows high;
And Dad, I ran from school this morning
— I had to — 'twas either that or cry'.
His Daddy didn't mind, his Mammy neither,
He stayed at home till Eastertime, and then
One morning he got dressed-up, took his schoolbag,
Brushed his hair, and went to school again.

He played with all the boys in *The Back Haggarts*,
A place that has no name (it's gone!) today,
High jumps, long jumps, triple jumps and marbles,
But there was one game not everyone could play —
The secret game that he was once allowed in:
Doctors, where you pulled down your pants
To be examined by one who was 'The Doctor';
Beebla ran when asked to drop his pants!
And they chased him, calling him 'a coward',
But Beebla didn't want to play that fun
(Mostly cos a girl was 'The Doctor'!)
He ran in home but didn't tell anyone.

And one time, too, he fought a boy for nothing
Cos the older boys had goaded them to fight;
After that, he never fought for nothing
Cos he knew inside himself it wasn't right.

Beebla would annoy you with his questions —
He wanted to know everything, and why:
Why he was, what was it to be *Beebla*,
And would his mother live, or would she die?
And what was it to die? Was it like *Cowboys*
Where you could live and die and live again?
Or would Mammy be forever up in Heaven?
(Forever was how much times one-to-ten?)

This was all before the television,
About the time we got electric light,
Before bungalows, bidets or flush-toilets,
Where dark was dark, and fairies roamed the night.
This story's a true story — *honest Injun*!
You tell me that it's funny, a bit sad;
Be happy! It has a happy ending
Cos Beebla grew up to be your Dad.

Gabriel Fitzmaurice

Down Our Street

Down our street lives a strange old man,
Heats his bed with a warming-pan,

Eats ice-cream in the middle of the night,
Reads in bed by candle-light,

Paddles in the gutter when the rain comes down,
Never, never, never goes shopping in town,

Goes out fishing if it's wet or fine
Hangs his wellies on the washing-line,

Sleeps outside when the weather's warm,
Rides his bike in a thunderstorm,

The happiest man you'll ever meet
Is my friend Ben from down our street.

June Crebbin

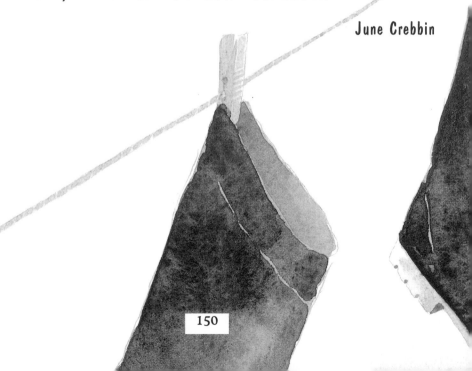

The Richest Poor Man in the Valley

On the outside
he seemed older than he was.
His face was like a weather map
full of bad weather
while inside
his heart was fat with sun.

With his two dogs
he cleared a thin silver path
across the Black Mountain.
And when winter
kicked in
they brought his sheep
down from the top
like sulky clouds.

Harry didn't care for things
that other people prize
like money, houses, bank accounts
and lies.
He was living in a caravan
until the day he died.

But at his funeral
his friends' tears
fell like a thousand
diamonds.

Lindsay MacRae

Grandad's Birthday Treat

It was me Grandad's birthday
we thought it a treat
to take him to restaurant for something to eat

We found this posh steakhouse
Grandad ordered a steak
a well done chewy-chunky beefcake
(I for one thought it was a dreadful mistake)

And no sooner he began to eat his meat
out jumped his false teeth
landing clean at his feet

Me mum gave me Grandad a family glare
'Grandad didn't I tell ye to have it
soft n' rare?
Grandad didn't turn the tiniest hair

He simply bent down and picked up his teeth
in no time again he was eating his meat
'What a feat,' he murmured quietly to his beard
'What a feat, Lord, bless the courage of my false teeth.'

Grace Nichols

152

Uncle Albert

When I was almost eight years old
My Uncle Albert came to stay;
He wore a watch-chain made of gold
And sometimes he would let me play
With both the chain and gleaming watch,
And though at times I might be rough
He never seemed to bother much.
He smelled of shaving-soap and snuff.
To me he was a kind of God,
Immensely wise and strong and kind,
And so I thought it rather odd
When I came home from school to find
Two strangers, menacing and tall,
In the parlour, looking grim
As Albert — suddenly quite small —
Let them rudely hustle him
Out to where a black car stood.
Both Albert and his
   watch and chain
Disappeared that
   day for good.
My parents said
   he'd gone to
   Spain.

Vernon Scannell

In Memory of My Mother

I do not think of you lying in the wet clay
Of a Monaghan graveyard; I see
You walking down a lane among the poplars
On your way to the station, or happily

Going to second Mass on a summer Sunday —
You meet me and you say:
'Don't forget to see about the cattle —'
Among your earthiest words the angels stray.

And I think of you walking along a headland
Of green oats in June,
So full of repose, so rich with life —
And I see us meeting at the end of a town

On a fair day by accident, after
The bargains are all made and we can walk
Together through the shops and stalls and markets
Free in the oriental streets of thought.

O you are not lying in the wet clay,
For it is a harvest evening now and we
Are piling up the ricks against the moonlight
And you smile up at us — eternally.

Patrick Kavanagh

Buying Winkles

My mother would spare me sixpence and say,
'Hurry up now and don't be talking to strange
men on the way.' I'd dash from the ghosts
on the stairs where the bulb had blown
out into Gardiner Street, all relief.
A bonus if the moon was in the strip of sky
between the tall houses, or stars out,
but even in rain I was happy — the winkles
would be wet and glisten blue like little
night skies themselves. I'd hold the tanner tight
and jump every crack in the pavement,
I'd wave up to women at sills or those
lingering in doorways and weave a glad path through
men heading out for the night.

She'd be sitting outside the Rosebowl Bar
on an orange-crate, a pram loaded
with pails of winkles before her.
When the bar doors swung open they'd leak
the smell of men together with drink
and I'd see light in golden mirrors.
I envied each soul in the hot interior.

I'd ask her again to show me the right way
to do it. She'd take a pin from her shawl —
'Open the eyelid. So. Stick it in
till you feel a grip, then slither him out.
Gently, mind.' The sweetest extra winkle

that brought the sea to me.
'Tell yer Ma I picked them fresh this morning.'

I'd bear the newspaper twists
bulging fat with winkles
proudly home, like torches.

Paula Meehan

155

The Fool in the Graveyard

When we die, we help each other out
Better than usual.

This was his big day, and he was glad
His Dad was dead, because everyone,
However important or usually
Unfriendly, came up to him and
Solemnly shook his new leather glove
And said 'I'm sorry for your trouble'.
No trouble at all. All these people
Who normally made fun of him
And said, 'What's your name, Dan?'
And laughed when he said 'Dan' (wasn't
That right and polite?), were nice as pie
Today. He'd missed him going to bed
But they'd given him a pound and
An apple and told him a joke.

That made him laugh a bit.
Coming down the aisle, he'd been
At the front with the coffin on
His shoulder, and everyone
Without exception looked straight
At him, some of them nodding gravely
Or mouthing 'How's Dan', and even
Crying, some of them. He'd tried
To smile and nod back, anxious
To encourage kindness. Maybe
They'd always be nice now, remembering
How he'd carried the coffin. Outside
It was very cold, but he had on
The Crombie coat his Dad had bought.

The earth was always yellower
Here than anywhere else, heaped
Next to the grave with its very
Straight sides. How did they dig

The sides so straight? The priest
Led the prayers, and he knew most
Of the answers. Things were looking up.
Today he was like the main actor
In the village play, or the footballer
Who took the frees, or the priest
On the altar. Every eye
Fixed on him! It was like being loved,
And he'd always wondered what that was like.
It wasn't embarrassing at all.

Bernard O'Donoghue

The Wild Trabler

The wild trabler the wild
trabler is a man dat fit when he is drunk
an ol ws shoten dat pepel tinkes he is ful of heat
But no gust a man dat life left be hind
a man hum never had a chanc in life since he wos born
on wonte out cast in hes on cuntrey senc he was a child
he was regetd leven wild lick the birds
ben hunted lick a wild anamel Pepel snar at hem
and a fard of hem Lif never brot hem aney hapnes
he corses the day he wos boorn He som times ask God
why he was put on ert he is a on happy man hum never had
a tru frend den he turns to the onley frend
he has, the frend dat makes hem laf and cry and happy
for whil. A frend dat wil breng hem tloser to det.
Dis a wild man

Nan Joyce

The Wild Traveller

The Wild Traveller. The wild traveller
Is a man that fights when he is drunk
And always shouting, that people think
He is full of hate. But no,
Just a man that life left behind
A man who never had a chance in life
Since he was born. Unwanted, outcast
In his own country since he was a child
He was rejected, living wild like the birds
Being hunted like a wild animal.
People snarl at him and are afraid of him
Life never brought him any happiness.
He curses the day he was born.
He sometimes asks God why he was put on earth.
He is an unhappy man who never had a true friend
Then he turns to the only friend he has. The friend
That makes him laugh and cry and happy for a while
A friend that will bring him closer to death.
This is a wild man.

version of 'The Wild Trabler' by Leland Bardwell

The Colour

*(The following lines are partly original, partly remembered
from a Wessex folk-rhyme)*

'What shall I bring you?
Please will white do
Best for your wearing
The long day through?'
'— White is for weddings,
Weddings, weddings,
White is for weddings,
And that won't do.'

'What shall I bring you?
Please will red do
The long day through?'
'— Red is for soldiers,
Soldiers, soldiers
Red is for soldiers
And that won't do.'

'What shall I bring you?
Please will blue do
Best for your wearing
The long day through?'
'— Blue is for sailors
Sailors, sailors
Blue is for sailors
And that won't do.'

'What shall I bring you?
Please will green do
Best for your wearing
The long day through?'
'— Green is for mayings,
Mayings, mayings
Green is for mayings,
And that won't do.'

'What shall I bring you
Then? Will black do
Best for your wearing
The long day through?'
'— Black is for mourning,
Mourning, mourning,
Black is for mourning,
And black will do.'

Thomas Hardy

Color

Wear it
Like a banner
For the proud —
Not like a shroud.
Wear it
Like a song
Soaring high —
Not moan or cry.

Langston Hughes

Caged Bird

A free bird leaps
on the back of the wind
and floats downstream
till the current ends
and dips his wing
in the orange sun rays
and dares to claim the sky.

But a bird that stalks
down his narrow cage
can seldom see through
his bars of rage
his wings are clipped and
his feet are tied
so he opens his throat to sing.

The caged bird sings
with a fearful trill
of things unknown
but longed for still
and his tune is heard
on the distant hill
for the caged bird
sings of freedom.

The free bird thinks of another breeze
and the trade winds soft through the sighing trees
and the fat worms waiting on a dawn-bright lawn
and he names the sky his own

But a caged bird stands on the grave of dreams
his shadow shouts on a nightmare scream
his wings are clipped and his feet are tied
so he opens his throat to sing.

The caged bird sings
with a tearful trill
of things unknown
but longed for still
and his tune is heard
on the distant hill
for the caged bird
sings of freedom.

Maya Angelou

Géibheann

Ainmhí mé

ainmhí allta
as na teochreasa
a bhfuil cliú agus cáil
ar mo scéimh

chroithfinn crainnte na coille
tráth
le mo gháir

ach anois
luím síos
agus breathnaím trí leathshúil
ar an gcrann aonraic sin thall

tagann na céadta daoine
chuile lá

a dhéanfadh rud ar bith
dom
ach mé a ligean amach

Caitlín Maude

Captivity

I am an animal

a wild animal
from the tropics
famous
for my beauty

I would shake the trees of the forest
once
with my cry

but now
I lie down
and observe with one eye
the lone tree yonder

people come in hundreds
every day
who would do anything
for me
but set me free

Géibheann translated by Gabriel Fitzmaurice

The Summer of Love

I went to sea in the Summer of Love
in a boat with my Boy Scout troop.
That summer I was only twelve,
our boat was a rusty sloop.

The island where we spent a week
lay twenty miles from home,
but in our minds we were refugees
from vaguely exotic doom.

A dozen boys who lolled about
on beaches, lied about girls,
stared at any passing yacht,
chanting the latest Beatles,

we liked the underwater voice
of 'Yellow Submarine' —
all the DJs ever chose
to play in the afternoon.

Our scoutmaster Mr. MacIntosh,
went quickly mad. He drank
from tidal pools and chased the fish
his eyes would never blink.

The fathers who came to take him away
in a little trawling boat
gave our troop permission to stay
three days with no adult.

With no adult, what savages
we were! Our boyish lies
grew like grotesques, the vestiges
of epic ecstasies!

But sometimes Mr. MacIntosh
came back in our fireside tales.
The world of grown-ups seemed awash
in trouble; took some pills,

some gassed themselves in their garages.
Recalling those who were mad,
we poked our sticks in the campfire's ashes,
unaccountably sad.

(Later I read that the Summer of Love
was the summer of the damned;
sixteen thousand American boys
had died in Viet Nam.)

We dreamed after girls on the passing yachts
and waited in the shade,
and when the adults came back in boats
to rescue us, we were glad.

On the wharf at home we bought ice cream cones,
shook the sand from our shoes.
We shambled back to casual lawns,
Monday meetings, other friends,
the feeling that summer never ends
and we would never lose.

David Mason

Dis Fighting

No more fighting please, why can't we stop dis fighting,
dis fighting hurting me, why don't we start uniting,
dem fighting in Angola, dem fighting in Manchester,
dem fighting in Jamaica, and dem fighting in Leicester,
well i might be black, my people were once slaves,
but time goes on, and loves come in,
so now we must behave,
it could be that you're white, and i live in your land,
no reason to make war, dis hard fe understand,
skinheads stop dis fighting,
rude boys stop dis fighting,
dreadlocks stop dis fighting,
we must start uniting,
our children should be happy and they should live as one,
we have to live together so let a love grow strong,
let us think about each other, there's no need to compete,
if two loves love each other then one love is complete,
no more fighting please, we have to stop dis fighting,
dis fighting hurting me, time fe start uniting,
dis fighting have no meaning, dis fighting is not fair,
dis fighting makes a profit for people who don't care,
no more fighting please, we have to stop, dis fighting,
dis fighting hurting me, the heathen love dis fighting.

Benjamin Zephaniah

Yobs

Me in the rain, my scooter broken down,
Fed up, pushing it, and these four lads
Block the pathway, jeering. Now, why's that?
No idea: for sure they don't know me.
I know them though (villages have eyes):
Petty vandals, go round daubing walls,
Snap the aerials off cars at night,
Wreck the children's playground, damage trees,
Tear the flowers up. Oh, I know them:
Know who's been expelled, in court. I know
Other things: I know who's unemployed,
Who come from broken homes, whose mother went,
Dumped him, four years old, to live with Gran.
I know who loiter now, unreachable,
By wasteland in the rainy winter dusk,
Who cry out 'Look at us!'
Not my affair.
I stand then, blocked, aggression's logan-stone
Poised, exquisite.
So, Who's leader? You,
Tall, in leather jacket, skull-adorned.
'Afternoon. You any good with these?
My baffle-pipe's gunged up, I've sheared the screw.'
Silence. Jacket boy considers me.
Thinking what? We've got a right one here?
Puzzled? Wary? I don't know. And then
'Hey, look, what you do ...' 'He needs ...' 'No look...'
Hands in concert, octopoidal, blurring,
Strip, clean out, refit. I clear my throat,
Fumble in my pocket, find two pounds.
'Look, I'd like ...' The leader, kneeling still,
Wipes his oily fingers, straightening,
Hesitates, then smiles and shakes his head.
The scooter starts first time. I ride away.

David Sutton

Before the Beginning

Sometimes in dreams I imagine
Alone and unafraid
I'm standing in the darkness
When the first bright stars were made.

When the sun sprang out of the blackness
And lit the world's first dawn
When torrents of rock rained upwards
And the mountains and seas were born.

And I'm there when the forest and meadows
Flowered for the very first time
When eyeless legless creatures
Oozed upwards out of the slime.

But when I awake and read the books
Though they tell me more and more
The one thing they never tell me
Is — what was there before ...

Gareth Owen

The Experts

Give three cheers for experts,
They know a thing or two,
And if we didn't have 'em
Whatever would we do?

They built a ship that couldn't sink;
It sailed across the sea.
Its name was the Titanic
It's gone down in history.

For years and years the experts knew
The Sun went round the Earth,
And when Copernicus said: 'Wrong!'
They couldn't hide their mirth.

They told Columbus not to sail
Because he might fall off.
They had King Louis bled to death,
Because he'd got a cough.

Lord Kelvin was a scientist —
A really clever guy,
Who proved by mathematics
That man would never fly.

And now we've all got nuclear power
So give three mighty cheers —
The experts say it can't go wrong
Once in ten thousand years!

Terry Jones

O, My Luve is Like a Red, Red Rose

O, my luve is like a red, red rose,
That's newly sprung in June:
O, my luve is like the melodie
That's sweetly played in tune.

As fair art thou, my bonnie lass,
So deep in luve am I;
And I will luve thee still, my dear,
Till a'[1] the seas gang[2] dry.

Till a' the seas gang dry, my dear,
And the rocks melt wi' the sun:
And I will luve thee still, my dear,
While the sands o' life shall run.

And fare thee weel,[3] my only luve,
And fare thee weel a while!
And I will come again, my luve,
Tho' it were ten thousand mile!

Robert Burns

1. a': all
2. gang: go
3. weel: well

Sonnet CXXX

My mistress' eyes are nothing like the sun;
Coral is far more red than her lips' red;
If snow be white, why then her breasts are dun;
If hairs be wires, black wires grow on her head.
I have seen roses damask'd, red and white,
But no such roses see I in her cheeks,
And in some perfumes is there more delight
Than in the breath that from my mistress reeks.
I love to hear her speak, yet well I know,
That music hath a far more pleasing sound.
I grant I never saw a goddess go;
My mistress when she walks treads on the ground.
And yet by heaven I think my love as rare
As any she belied with false compare.

William Shakespeare

173

Mo Ghrása (Idir Lúibíní)

Níl mo ghrása
ar bhláth na n-airní
a bhíonn i ngairdín
(nó ar chrann ar bith)

Is má tá aon ghaol aige
le nóiníní
is as a chluasa a fhásfaidh siad
(nuair a bheidh sé ocht dtroigh síos)

Ní haon ghlaise cheolmhar
iad a shúile
(táid róchóngarach dá chéile
ar an gcéad dul síos)

Is más slim é síoda
tá ribí a ghruaige
(mar bhean dhubh Shakespeare)
ina WIRE deilgneach

Ach is cuma san.
Tugann sé dom
úlla
(is nuair a bhíonn sé i ndea-ghiúmar
caora fíniúna)

Nuala Ní Dhomhnaill

My Love (In Parenthesis)

My love is nothing like
the blossom on the sloe
that grows in the garden
(or on any tree)

and if he's related
to the daisies
it's from his ears they'll grow
(when he's eight feet underground)

no singing stream
his eyes
(they're set too close together
to begin with)

and if silk be smooth
the ribs of his hair
(like Shakespeare's Dark Lady)
are thorny wire

But no matter.
He gives me
apples
(and when he's in humour
grapes)

'Mo Ghrása (Idir Lúibíní)'
translated from the Irish by Gabriel Fitzmaurice

She Neither Turned Away...

She neither turned away, nor yet began
To speak harsh words, nor did she bar the door;
But looked at him who was her love before
As if he were an ordinary man.

'Amaru' translated from the Sanskrit
by John Brough

A Bunch of Thyme

Come all you maidens young and fair,
All you that are blooming in your prime.
Oh always beware
And keep your garden fair.
Let no man steal away your thyme.

Chorus
For thyme it is a precious thing
And thyme brings all things to my mind.
Oh thyme with all its labours
Along with all its joys,
Thyme brings all things to my mind.

Oh once I had a bunch of thyme,
I thought it never would decay,
But on came a lusty sailor
Who chanced to pass that way.
He stole my bunch of thyme away.

The sailor gave to me a rose
A rose that never will decay.
He gave it to me
To keep me well minded
Of when he stole my thyme away.

So come all you maidens young and fair,
All you that are blooming in your prime,
Oh always beware
And keep your garden fair.
Let no man steal away your thyme.

Chorus
For thyme it is a precious thing
And thyme brings all things to my mind.
Oh thyme with all its labours
Along with all its joys,
Thyme brings all things to my mind.

Traditional

Leisure

What is this life if, full of care,
We have no time to stand and stare.

No time to stand beneath the boughs
And stare as long as sheep or cows.

No time to see, when woods we pass,
Where squirrels hide their nuts in grass.

No time to see, in broad daylight,
Streams full of stars like skies at night.

No time to turn at Beauty's glance,
And watch her feet, how they can dance.

No time to wait till her mouth can
Enrich that smile her eyes began.

A poor life this if, full of care,
We have no time to stand and stare.

W.H. Davies

The Vastest Things are Those We May Not Learn

The vastest things are those we may not learn.
We are not taught to die, nor to be born,
Nor how we burn
With love
How pitiful is our enforced return
To those small things we are the masters of.

Mervyn Peake

The Red Wheelbarrow

so much depends
upon

a red wheel
barrow

glazed with rain
water

beside the white
chickens.

William Carlos Williams

Fern

There is no lesson in the fern
except uncurling slowly,
one green frond at a time;
learning to do well
in dark places;
letting growth come
from the underside of things.

Kathleen Cain

Botany

Duckweed

Afloat on their own reflection, these leaves
With roots that reach only part of the way,
Will fall asleep at the end of summer,
Draw in their skirts and sink to the bottom.

Foxglove

Though the corolla dangles upside down,
Nothing ever falls out, neither nectar
Nor loosening pollen grains: a thimble,
Stall for the little finger and the bee.

Dock

Its green flowers attract only the wind
But a red vein may irrigate the leaf
And blossom into blush or birthmark
Or a remedy for the nettle's sting.

Orchid

The tuber absorbs summer and winter,
Its own ugly shape, twisted arms and legs,
A recollection of the heart, one artery
Sprouting upwards to support a flower.

Michael Longley

The Daffodils

I wandered lonely as a cloud
That floats on high o'er vales and hills,
When all at once I saw a crowd,
A host, of golden daffodils;
Beside the lake, beneath the trees,
Fluttering and dancing in the breeze.

Continuous as the stars that shine
And twinkle on the milky way,
They stretched in never-ending line
Along the margin of a bay:
Ten thousand saw I at a glance,
Tossing their heads in sprightly dance.

The waves beside them danced; but they
Out-did the sparkling waves in glee:
A poet could not but be gay,
In such a jocund company:
I gazed — and gazed — but little thought
What wealth the show to me had brought:

For oft, when on my couch I lie
In vacant or in pensive mood,
They flash upon that inward eye
Which is the bliss of solitude;
And then my heart with pleasure fills,
And dances with the daffodils.

William Wordsworth

The Poem I'd Like to Write

I'd like to write a poem about daffodils.
I'd like to say
How beautiful they look on a March day,
Their green stems rising
Into those large, incredibly surprising
Trumpets of pure gold;
And how, after frost and cold,
They bring
Such colour and such warmth to everything,
They shake us into Spring.

I'd like to write it, but I know
That Wordsworth wrote it long ago.

Clive Samson

The Daffodils

Your daughter is reading to you over and over again
Wordsworth's 'The Daffodils', her lips at your ear.
She wants you to know what a good girl you have been.
You are so good at joined-up writing the page you
Have filled with your knowledge is completely black.
Your hand presses her hand in response to rhyme words.
She wants you to turn away from the wooden desk
Before you die, and look out of the classroom window
Where all the available space is filled with daffodils.

Michael Longley

The Lake Isle of Innisfree

I will arise and go now, and go to Innisfree,
And a small cabin build there, of clay and wattles made:
Nine bean-rows will I have there, a hive for the honey-bee,
And live alone in the bee-loud glade.

And I shall have some peace there, for peace comes dropping slow,
Dropping from the veils of the morning to where the cricket sings;
There midnight's all a glimmer, and noon a purple glow,
And evening full of the linnet's wings.

I will arise and go now, for always night and day
I hear lake water lapping with low sounds by the shore;
While I stand on the roadway, or on the pavements grey,
I hear it in the deep heart's core.

William Butler Yeats

He Refuses to Read his Public's Favourite Poem

*'I think Yeats hated all his early poems, and 'Innisfree' most of all. One evening
I begged him to read it. A look of tortured irritation came into his face and
continued there until the reading was over'*
Dorothy Wellesley

They always asked for it. He knew they would.
They knew it off by heart: a b, a b,
Reliable rhymes; thoughts they could understand.
But dreams, as well. Their own, their Innisfree.

So why refuse? He knew the rest were better,
His serious bid for immortality.
What man defends the tenets of his twenties?
Who would be tied for life to Innisfree?

'Give us Arise and go in your Irish accent,
Give us the cabin, the glade, the beans, the bees.
Not Maud, Byzantium, Crazy Jane, Cuchulain.
We are your public. Give us more Innisfrees.'

'A poem heard twelve times in public is dead and finished.'
'Ah no! Too much of a good thing there cannot be.
Too much of Shakespeare, Wordsworth, Milton, Shelley,
There is. But not enough of Innisfree.

I will arise and go now — Senator,[1] please!'
'I won't. I can't. I'm not him any more.
Young fool who prattles of crickets and wattles and linnets —
I hate him in the deep heart's core.'

U.A. Fanthorpe

1. Senator: Yeats was a member of the Irish Senate.

Waterfall

What message do you bring me
Waterfall?
What songs do you sing me
Waterfall?
Songs of other days
Lovely lingering lays
Living on always
Waterfall.

Say what is your duty
Waterfall?
Just to roll along in beauty
Waterfall.
From the rocky cliffs to bound
Flinging music all around
In the thunder of your sound
Waterfall.

Do you remember long ago,
Waterfall,
And the friends we used to know
Waterfall?
Here in youth they loved to stray
But they're dead or far away
And I come alone today
Waterfall.

Do you really love to play
Waterfall,
And dance in silver spray
Waterfall?
I see you decked with foam
As onward still you roam
To seek your ocean home
Waterfall.

We are much akin in ways
Waterfall,
Moving forward all our days
Waterfall,
'Til our spirits shall be free
In the everlasting sea
For all Eternity
Waterfall.

Dan Keane

The Inchcape Rock

No stir in the air, no stir in the sea,
The ship was still as she could be,
Her sails from heaven received no motion,
Her keel was steady in the ocean.

Without either sign or sound of their shock
The waves flow'd over the Inchcape Rock;
So little they rose, so little they fell,
They did not move the Inchcape Bell.

The holy abbot of Aberbrothok
Had placed that bell on the Inchcape Rock;
On a buoy in the storm it floated and swung,
And over the waves its warning rung.

When the Rock was hid by the surge's swell,
The mariners heard the warning bell;
And then they knew the perilous Rock,
And blest the Abbot of Aberbrothok.

The Sun in heaven was shining gay,
All things were joyful on that day;
The sea-birds scream'd as they wheel'd round,
And there was joyance in their sound.

The buoy of the Inchcape Bell was seen
A darker speck on the ocean green;
Sir Ralph the Rover walk'd his deck,
And he fixed his eye on the darker speck.

He felt the cheering power of spring,
It made him whistle, it made him sing,
His heart was mirthful to excess,
But the Rover's mirth was wickedness.

His eye was on the Inchcape float;
Quoth he, 'My men, put out the boat,
And row me to the Inchcape Rock,
And I'll plague the Abbot of Aberbrothok.'

The boat is lower'd, the boatmen row,
And to the Inchcape Rock they go;
Sir Ralph bent over from the boat,
And he cut the bell from the Inchcape float.

188

Down sunk the bell with a gurgling sound,
The bubbles rose and burst around;
Quoth Sir Ralph, 'The next who comes to the Rock
Won't bless the Abbot of Aberbrothok.'

Sir Ralph the Rover sail'd away,
He scour'd the seas for many a day;
And now grown rich with plunder'd store,
He steers his course for Scotland's shore.

So thick a haze o'erspreads the sky
They cannot see the Sun on high;
The wind hath blown a gale all day,
At evening it hath died away.

On the deck the Rover takes his stand,
So dark it is they see no land.
Quoth Sir Ralph, 'It will be lighter soon,
For there is the dawn of the rising Moon'.

'Canst hear', said one, 'the breakers roar?
For methinks we should be near the shore.'
'Now where we are I cannot tell,
But I wish I could hear the Inchcape Bell.'

They hear no sound, the swell is strong;
Though the wind hath fallen they drift along,
Till the vessel strikes with a shivering shock —
'Oh Christ! It is the Inchcape Rock!'

Sir Ralph the Rover tore his hair;
He curst himself in his despair;
The waves rush in on every side,
The ship is sinking beneath the tide.

But even in his dying fear
One dreadful sound could the Rover hear,
A sound as if with the Inchcape Bell,
The Devil below was ringing his knell.

Robert Southey

maggie and milly and molly and may

maggie and milly and molly and may
went down to the beach (to play one day)

and maggie discovered a shell that sang
so sweetly she couldn't remember her troubles, and

milly befriended a stranded star
whose rays five languid fingers were;

and molly was chased by a horrible thing
which raced sideways while blowing bubbles: and

may came home with a smooth round stone
as small as a world and as large as alone.

For whatever we lose (like a you or a me)
it's always ourselves we find in the sea

E.E. Cummings

190

Tell Me, Tell Me, Sarah Jane

Tell me, tell me, Sarah Jane,
Tell me, dearest daughter,
Why are you holding in your hand
A thimbleful of water?
Why do you hold it to your eye
And gaze both late and soon
From early morning light until
The rising of the moon?

Mother, I hear the mermaids cry,
I hear the mermen sing,
And I can see the sailing-ships
All made of sticks and string.
And I can see the jumping fish,
The whales that fall and rise
And swim about the waterspout
That swarms up to the skies.

Tell me, tell me, Sarah Jane,
Tell your darling mother,
Why do you walk beside the tide
As though you loved none other?
Why do you listen to a shell
And watch the billows curl,
And throw away your diamond ring
And wear instead the pearl?

Mother I hear the water
Beneath the headland pinned,
And I can see the sea-gull
Sliding down the wind.
I taste the salt upon my tongue
As sweet as sweet can be.

Tell me, my dear, whose voice do you hear?

It is the sea, the sea.

Charles Causley

Changes

Once the rivers were ballads
but now they're forgotten music.
Once the tiger was an emperor
but now it's moth-eaten.
Once the whale was a metropolis
but now it's a sunken city.
Once the trees were cathedrals
but now they're without faith.
Once the Inuit was a survivor
but now he's been thawed out.
Once the soil was a banquet
but now it's forcefed.
Once the rain was a husband
but now it's a gangster.
Once the world was a berry
but now it's all thorns.

Norman Silver

Ozymandias

I met a traveller from an antique land
Who said: Two vast and trunkless legs of stone
Stand in the desert ... Near them, on the sand,
Half sunk, a shattered visage lies, whose frown,
And wrinkled lip, and sneer of cold command,
Tell that its sculptor well those passions read
Which yet survive, stamped on these lifeless things,
The hand that mocked them, and the heart that fed:
And on the pedestal these words appear:
'My name is Ozymandias, king of kings:
Look on my works, ye Mighty, and despair!'
Nothing beside remains. Round the decay
Of that colossal wreck, boundless and bare
The lone and level sands stretch far away.

Percy Bysshe Shelley

I'll Tell Me Ma

I'll tell me Ma when I go home
The boys won't leave the girls alone
They pulled me hair and stole me comb
But that's all right till I go home;
She is handsome, she is pretty,
She's the belle of Belfast City,
She's a-courting one-two-three,
Please won't you tell me who is she.

Albert Mooney says he loves her,
All the boys are fighting for her,
They rap at the door and they ring at the bell,
Saying, 'Oh, my true love, are you well?'
Out she comes as white as snow,
Rings on her fingers, bells on her toes,
Old Johnny Murray says she'll die,
If she doesn't get the fellow with the roving eye.

Let the wind and the rain and the hail blow high
And the snow come travelling from the sky,
She's as nice as apple-pie,
And she'll get her own lad bye and bye.
When she gets a lad of her own,
She won't tell her ma when she gets home,
Let them all come as they will,
But it's Albert Mooney she loves still.

Traditional

194

Will Ye Go, Lassie, Go?

Oh, the summertime is coming
And the trees are sweetly blooming
And the wild mountain thyme grows
Around the blooming heather,
Will ye go, lassie, go?

Chorus
And we'll all go together
To pluck wild mountain thyme,
All around the blooming heather,
Will ye go, lassie, go?

I will build my love a tower
Near yon pure crystal fountain,
And on it I will pile
All the flowers of the mountain,
Will ye go, lassie, go?

Chorus
And we'll all go together
To pluck wild mountain thyme,
All around the blooming heather,
Will ye go, lassie, go?

If my true love she were gone,
I would surely find another,
Where wild mountain thyme grows
Around the blooming heather,
Will ye go, lassie, go?

Chorus
And we'll all go together
To pluck wild mountain thyme,
All around the blooming heather,
Will ye go, lassie, go?

Traditional

Soldier, Soldier

'Oh! Soldier, soldier, won't you marry me,
With your musket, fife and drum?'
'Oh no, sweet maid, I cannot marry thee,
For I have no coat to put on.'

So up she went to her grandfather's chest,
And she got him a coat of the very, very best
And the soldier put it on!

'Oh! Soldier, soldier, won't you marry me,
With your musket, fife and drum?'
'Oh no, sweet maid, I cannot marry thee,
For I have no hat to put on.'

So up she went to her grandfather's chest,
And she got him a hat of the very, very best
And the soldier put it on!

'Oh! Soldier, soldier, won't you marry me,
With your musket, fife and drum?'
'Oh no, sweet maid, I cannot marry thee,
For I have no boots to put on.'

So up she went to her grandfather's chest,
And she got him a pair of the very, very best
And the soldier put them on!

'Oh! Soldier, soldier, won't you marry me,
With your musket, fife and drum?'
'Oh no, sweet maid, I cannot marry thee,
For I have a wife of my own!'

Traditional

Dirty Old Town

I found my love by the gas works cross,
Dreamed a dream by the old canal,
Kissed my girl, by the factory wall,
Dirty old town, dirty old town.

I heard a siren from the dock,
Saw a train set the night on fire,
Smelled the spring on the smoky wind,
Dirty old town, dirty old town.

Clouds are drifting across the moon,
Cats are prowling on their beat,
Springs a girl in the street at night
Dirty old town, dirty old town.

I'm going to make a good sharp axe,
Shining steel, tempered in the fire,
We'll chop you down like an old dead tree,
Dirty old town, dirty old town.

Ewan McColl

Plane Wreck at Los Gatos

This song is about the death of twenty-eight Mexican migrant
deportees in a crash near Coalinga, California, 1948.

The crops are all in and the peaches are rottening
The oranges are piled in their creosote dumps;
You're flying them back to the Mexico border
To pay all their money to wade back again.

Good-bye to my Juan, Good-bye Rosalita;
Adios muy amigo, Jesus and Marie,
You won't have a name when you ride the big airplane
All they will call you will be deportees.

My father's own father he waded that river;
They took all the money he made in his life;
My brothers and sisters come working the fruit trees
And they rode the truck till they took down and died.

Good-bye to my Juan, Good-bye Rosalita;
Adios muy amigo, Jesus and Marie,
You won't have a name when you ride the big airplane
All they will call you will be deportees.

Some of us are illegal and some are not wanted,
Our work contract's out and we have to move on;
Six hundred miles to that Mexico border,
They chase us like outlaws, like rustlers, like thieves.

Good-bye to my Juan, Good-bye Rosalita;
Adios muy amigo, Jesus and Marie,
You won't have a name when you ride the big airplane
All they will call you will be deportees.

We died in your hills, we died in your deserts,
We died in your valleys and died on your plains;
We died neath your trees and we died in your bushes,
Both sides of this river we died just the same.

Good-bye to my Juan, Good-bye Rosalita;
Adios muy amigo, Jesus and Marie,
You won't have a name when you ride the big airplane
All they will call you will be deportees.

The sky plane caught fire over Los Gatos Canyon,
A fireball of lightning and shook all our hills.
Who are all these friends all scattered like dry leaves?
The radio says they are just deportees.

Good-bye to my Juan, Good-bye Rosalita;
Adios muy amigo, Jesus and Marie,
You won't have a name when you ride the big airplane
All they will call you will be deportees.

Is this the best way we can grow our big orchards?
Is this the best way we can grow our good fruit?
To fall like dry leaves to rot on my top soil
And be called by no name except deportees?

Good-bye to my Juan, Good-bye Rosalita;
Adios muy amigo, Jesus and Marie,
You won't have a name when you ride the big airplane
All they will call you will be deportees.

Woody Guthrie

Black is the Colour

But black is the colour of my true love's hair,
Her cheeks are like some roses fair,
The prettiest eyes and the neatest hands,
I love the ground whereon she stands.

I love my love and well she knows,
I love the ground whereon she goes,
If you no more on earth I see
I won't serve you as you have me.

The winter's passed and the leaves are green,
The time is passed that we have seen,
But still I hope the time will come
When you and I shall be as one.

I go to the Clyde for to mourn and weep,
But satisfied I never could sleep,
I'll write you a letter in a few short lines,
I'll suffer death ten thousand times.

So fare you well, my own true love,
The time has passed, but I wish you well,
But still I hope the time will come
When you and I will be as one.

I love my love and well she knows,
I love the ground whereon she goes,
The prettiest face and the neatest hands,
I love the ground whereon she stands.

Traditional

Sea Fever

I must go down to the seas again, to the lonely sea and the sky,
And all I ask is a tall ship and a star to steer her by;
And the wheel's kick and the wind's song and the white sail's shaking,
And a grey mist on the sea's face and a grey dawn breaking.

I must go down to the seas again, for the call of the running tide
Is a wild call and a clear call that may not be denied;
And all I ask is a windy day with the white clouds flying,
And the flung spray and the blown spume, and the sea-gulls crying.

I must go down to the seas again, to the vagrant gipsy life,
To the gull's way and the whale's way, where the wind's like a whetted knife;
And all I ask is a merry yarn from a laughing fellow-rover,
And quiet sleep and a sweet dream when the long trick's over.

John Masefield

The North Ship

I saw three ships go sailing by,
Over the sea, the lifting sea,
And the wind rose in the mourning sky,
And one was rigged for a long journey.

The first ship turned towards the west,
Over the sea, the running sea,
And by the wind was all possessed
And carried to a rich country.

The second turned towards the east,
Over the sea, the quaking sea,
And the wind hunted it like a beast
To anchor in captivity.

The third ship drove towards the north,
Over the sea, the darkening sea,
But no breath of wind came forth,
And the decks shone frostily.

The northern sky rose high and black
Over the proud unfruitful sea,
East and west the ships came back
Happily or unhappily:

But the third went wide and far
Into an unforgiving sea
Under a fire-spilling star,
And it was rigged for a long journey.

Philip Larkin

Sailor

My sweetheart's a Sailor,
He sails on the sea,
When he comes home
He brings presents for me;
Coral from China,
Silks from Siam,
Parrots and pearls
From Seringapatam,
Silver from Mexico,
Gold from Peru,
Indian feathers
From Kalamazoo,
Scents from Sumatra,
Mantillas from Spain,
A fisherman's float
From the waters of Maine,
Reindeers from Lapland,
Ducks from Bombay,
A unicorn's horn
From the Land of Cathay —
Isn't it lucky
For someone like me
To marry a Sailor
Who sails on the sea!

Eleanor Farjeon

Nursery Rhyme of Innocence and Experience

I had a silver penny
And an apricot tree
And I said to the sailor
On the white quay

'Sailor O sailor
Will you bring me
If I give you my penny
And my apricot tree

A fez from Algeria
An Arab drum to beat
A little gilt sword
And a parakeet?'

And he smiled and he kissed me
As strong as death
And I saw his red tongue
And I felt his sweet breath

'You may keep your penny
And your apricot tree
And I'll bring your presents
Back from sea.'

O the ship dipped down
On the rim of the sky
And I waited while three
Long summers went by

Then one steel morning
On the white quay
I saw a grey ship
Come in from the sea

Slowly she came
Across the bay
For her flashing rigging
Was shot away

All round her wake
The seabirds cried
And flew in and out
Of the hole in her side

Slowly she came
In the path of the sun
And I heard the sound
Of a distant gun

And a stranger came running
Up to me
From the deck of the ship
And he said, said he

'O are you the boy
Who would wait on the quay
With the silver penny
And the apricot tree?

'I've a plum-coloured fez
And a drum for thee
And a sword and a parakeet
From over the sea.'

O where is the sailor
With bold red hair?
And what is that volley
On the bright air?

O where are the other
Girls and boys?
And why have you brought me
Children's toys?'

Charles Causley

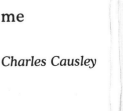

The Juggler's Wife

Last night, in front of thousands of people,
he placed a pencil on his nose
and balanced a chair upright on it
while he spun a dozen plates behind his back.
Then he slowly stood on his head to read a book
at the same time as he transferred the lot
to the big toe of his left foot.
They said it was impossible.

This morning, in our own kitchen,
I ask him to help with the washing-up —
so he gets up, knocks over a chair,
trips over the cat, swears, drops the tray
and smashes the whole blooming lot!
You wouldn't think it was possible.

Cicely Herbert

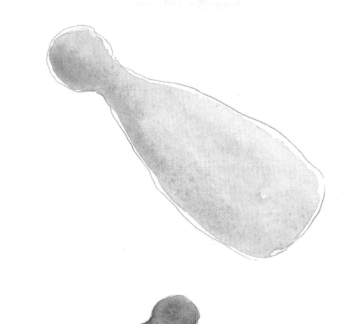

Sunday Night in Santa Rosa

The carnival is over. The high tents,
the palaces of light, are folded flat
and trucked away. A three-time loser yanks
the Wheel of Fortune off the wall. Mice
pick through the garbage by the popcorn stand.
A drunken giant falls asleep beside
the juggler, and the Dog-Faced Boy sneaks off
to join the Serpent Lady for the night.
Wind sweeps ticket stubs along the walk.
The Dead Man loads his coffin on a truck.
Off in a trailer by the parking lot
the radio predicts tomorrow's weather
while a clown stares in a dressing mirror,
takes out a box, and peels away his face.

Dana Gioia

Poetry Doesn't Pay

People keep telling me
Your poems, you know,
you've really got something there,
I mean really.

When the rent man calls, I go
down on my knees, and through
the conscience box I tell him.

This is somebody speaking,
short distance, did you know
I have something here with my poems?
People keep telling me.

'All I want is fourteen pounds
and ten pence, hold the poesy.'

But you don't realise
I've got something here.

'If you don't come across
with fourteen pounds and ten pence soon
you'll have something at the side of the road,
made colourful by a little snow.'

But.

'But nothing,
you can't pay me in poems or prayers
or with your husband's jokes,
or with photographs of your children
in lucky lemon sweaters
hand-made by your dead Grand Aunt
who had amnesia and the croup.

I'm from the corporation,
what do we know or care about poesy,
much less grand amnostic dead aunts.'

But people keep telling me.

'They lie.

If you don't have fourteen pounds
and ten pence, you have nothing
but the light of the penurious moon.'

Rita Ann Higgins

Mise Raifterí

Mise Raifterí an file,
Lán dóchais is grá,
Le súile gan solas,
Le ciúneas gan chrá.

Dul siar ar m'aistear
Le solas mo chroí,
Fann agus tuirseach
Go deireadh mo shlí.

Féach anois mé
Is mo chúl le balla
Ag seinm cheoil
Do phócaí folamh.

Antoine Ó Reachtabhra (Raifterí)

I Am Raftery

I am Raftery the poet
Of hope and love,
With eyes without light
Calm, untroubled.

In the light of my heart
Retracing my way,
Worn and weary
To the end of my days.

Look at me now,
My back to the wall,
Playing music,
For empty-pockets.

*'Mise Raifterí' translated from the Irish
by Gabriel Fitzmaurice*

Windsong

I am the seed
that grew the tree
that gave the wood
to make the page
to fill the book
with poetry.

Judith Nicholls

Ceist na Teangan

Cuirim mo dhóchas ar snámh
i mbáidín teangan
faoi mar a leagfá naíonán
i gcliabhán
a bheadh fite fuaite
de dhuilleoga feileastraim
is bitiúman agus pic
bheith cuimilte lena thóin

ansan é a leagadh síos
i measc na ngiolcach
is coigeal na mban sí
le taobh na habhann,
féachaint n'fheadaraís
cá dtabharfaidh an sruth é,
féachaint, dála Mhaoise,
an bhfóirfidh iníon Fharoinn?

Nuala Ní Dhomhnaill

The Language Issue

I place my hope on the water
in this little boat
of the language, the way a body might put
an infant

in a basket of intertwined
iris leaves,
its underside proofed
with bitumen and pitch,

then set the whole thing down amidst
the sedge
and bulrushes by the edge
ofa river

only to have it borne hither and thither,
not knowing where it might end up;
in the lap, perhaps,
of some Pharaoh's daughter.

'Ceist na Teangan' translated from the Irish
by Paul Muldoon

The Country Fiddler

My uncle played the fiddle — more elegantly the violin —
A favourite at barn and crossroads dance,
He knew The Sailor's Bonnet and The Fowling Piece.

Bachelor head of a house full of sisters,
Runner of poor racehorses, spendthrift,
He left for the New World in an old disgrace.

He left his fiddle in the rafters
When he sailed, never played afterwards;
A rural art silenced in the discord of Brooklyn.

A heavily-built man, tranquil-eyed as an ox,
He ran a wild speakeasy, and died of it.
During the Depression many dossed in his cellar.

I attended his funeral in the Church of the Redemption,
Then, unexpected successor, reversed time
To return where he had been born.

During my schooldays the fiddle rusted
(The bridge fell away, the catgut snapped)
Reduced to a plaything stinking of stale rosin.

The country people asked if I also had music
(All the family had had) but the fiddle was in pieces
And the rafters remade, before I discovered my craft.

Twenty years afterwards, I saw the church again,
And promised to remember my burly godfather
And his rural craft, after this fashion:

So succession passes, through strangest hands.

John Montague

And Now Goodbye

To all those million verses in the world
I've added just a few.
They probably were no wiser than a cricket's chirrup.
I know. Forgive me.
I'm coming to the end.

They weren't even the first footmarks
in the lunar dust.
If at times they sparkled after all
it was not their light.
I loved this language.

And that which forces silent lips
to quiver
will make young lovers kiss
as they stroll through red-gilded fields
under a sunset
slower than in the tropics.

Poetry is with us from the start.
Like loving,
like hunger, like the plague, like war.
At times my verses were embarrassingly foolish.

But I make no excuse.
I believe that seeking beautiful words
is better
than killing and murdering.

Jaroslav Seifert
Translated by Ewald Osers

Everything is Going to be All Right

How should I not be glad to contemplate
the clouds clearing beyond the dormer window
and a high tide reflected on the ceiling?
There will be dying, there will be dying,
but there is no need to go into that.
The poems flow from the hand unbidden
and the hidden source is the watchful heart.
The sun rises in spite of everything
and the far cities are beautiful and bright.
I lie here in a riot of sunlight
watching the day break and the clouds flying.
Everything is going to be all right.

Derek Mahon

Poetry Acknowledgements

For permission to reprint poems in this anthology, we would like to acknowledge the following with thanks. For poems by

John Agard, 'Hatch Me a Riddle' from *Laughter is an Egg* published by Viking 1990 and 'Into the Unknown' from *Get Back, Pimple!* Viking 1996, by kind permission of John Agard c/o Caroline Sheldon Literary Agency.

Allan Ahlberg, 'The Ghost Teacher' from *Heard it in the Playground* by Allan Ahlberg (Viking, 1989), copyright Allan Ahlberg 1989. Reproduced by permission of Penguin Books Ltd.

Jez Alborough, 'A Smile' from *Shake Before Opening*, Hutchinson Children's Books.

Amaru, 'She Neither Turned Away...' from *Poems from the Sanskrit* translated by John Brough (Penguin Classics, 1968) copyright (c) John Brough, 1968. Reproduced by permission of Penguin Books Ltd.

Maya Angelou, 'Caged Bird' from *The Complete Collected Poems* by Maya Angelou, Virago Press.

W.H. Auden, 'O What is that Sound' from *W.H. Auden: Collected Poems*, edited by Edward Mendelson, copyright 1937 and renewed 1965 by W.H. Auden, reprinted by permission of Random House Inc.

Leland Bardwell, 'The Wild Traveller' version of 'The Wild Trabler' from *Irish Poetry Now*, Wolfhound Press.

James Berry, 'Riddle Poems' and 'One' from *When I Dance*, reproduced courtesy of Peters Fraser & Dunlop.

Eavan Boland, 'Night Feed' from *Selected Poems*, Carcanet Press Ltd.

Margot Bosonnet, 'Mammy said' from *Skyscraper Ted*, Wolfhound Press, courtesy of the author.

Kathleen Cain, 'Fern', courtesy of the author.

Charles Causley, 'I Saw a Jolly Hunter' and 'Nursery Rhyme of Innocence and Experience' from *Collected Poems*, 'Miller's End' and 'Tell Me, Tell Me, Sarah Jane' from *Figgie Hobbin & Other Poems*, Macmillan.

Leonard Clark, 'First Primrose' and 'Snail', courtesy of the Literary Executor of Leonard Clark.

Wendy Cope, 'Kenneth' from *Uncollected Poems*, courtesy of the author.

June Crebbin, 'Cathedral' and 'River' from *Cows Moo, Cars Toot!* by June Crebbin (Viking, 1995) copyright (c) June Crebbin 1995; 'Down Our Street' and 'Penguin' from *The Dinosaur's Dinner*, by June Crebbin (Viking, 1992) copyright (c) June Crebbin 1992; 'Kite' from *The Jungle Sale* by June Crebbin (Viking Kestrel, 1988) copyright (c) June Crebbin 1998.

Iain Crichton-Smith, 'The Rainbow' from *Collected Poems*, Carcanet Press Ltd.

E.E. Cummings, 'little tree', 'maggie and milly and molly and may' and 'rain or hail' are reprinted from *Complete Poems 1904–1962* by E.E. Cummings, edited by George J. Firmage, by permission of W.W. Norton & Company Ltd. Copyright (c) 1991 by the Trustees for the E.E. Cummings Trust and George James Firmage.

W.H. Davies, 'Leisure' from *Selected Poems*, courtesy of the Executors of W.H. Davies and Random House.

Walter De La Mare, 'The Listeners' from *Collected Rhymes and Verses*, courtesy of the Estate of Walter De La Mare.

Lee Dellow, 'Computer Games' from *Techno Talk*, ed. Trevor Harvey, Bodley Head.

Peter Dixon, 'Colour of My Dreams' from *Kingfisher Book of Comic Verse*, courtesy of the author.

Berlie Doherty, 'The Deserted Village' from *Walking on Air*, Harper Collins, courtesy of the author.

Ann Drysdale, 'Winter Song', copyright Ann Drysdale from *The Turn of the Cucumber* (1995) reproduced by permission of Peterloo Poets.

Richard Edwards, '? ? ?' and 'Useless Things' from *A Mouse in my Roof*, copyright Richard Edwards 1988, 'Tall Paul' from *The House That Caught Cold* copyright Richard Edwards 1991; reproduced by permission of Felicity Bryan and the author. A

Mouse in My Roof was first published in the UK by Orchard Books, a division of the Watts Publishing Group, 96 Leonard Street, London EC2A 4RH. 'When I Was Three' from *The Word Party*, Lutterworth Press.

D.J. Enright, 'Blue Umbrellas' from *Collected Poems 1948–1998*, Oxford University Press, courtesy of the author.

U.A. Fanthorpe, 'He Refuses to Read his Public's Favourite Poem'. Copyright U.A. Fanthorpe from *Safe As Houses* (1995), reproduced by permission of Peterloo Poets.

Eleanor Farjeon, 'For Them'. Copyright (c) Eleanor Farjeon from *Silver Sand and Snow* (Michael Joseph) and 'Sailor' copyright (c) Eleanor Farjeon from *Then There Were Three* (Michael Joseph).

Vicki Feaver, 'Crab Apple Jelly', and 'Slow Reader', Random House.

Gyözö Ferencz, 'Dream and Forgetting', translated by George Szirtes, courtesy of the author.

Gabriel Fitzmaurice, 'Beebla' from *But Dad!* Poolbeg, and the following translations: 'A Change', 'Captivity', 'Christmas Eve', 'Daddy-Long-Legs', 'I Am Raftery', 'Look', 'My Love (In Parenthesis)', 'Television', 'The Dignity of Grief', 'The Pig', 'The Trout', all courtesy of the author.

Robin Flower, translation of 'Pangur Bán' courtesy of *The Lilliput Press*, Dublin.

Robert Frost, 'Stopping by Woods on a Snowy Evening' from *The Poetry of Robert Frost* edited by Edward Connery Latham, courtesy of the Estate of Robert Frost, the editor and Jonathan Cape.

Dana Gioia, 'Sunday Night in Santa Rosa' from *Daily Horoscope*, courtesy of the author.

Woody Guthrie, 'Plane Wreck at Los Gatos', Vanguard Records.

Mike Harding, 'Train by Skerries' from *Buns for the Elephants* by Mike Harding (Viking 1995) copyright (c) Mike Harding, 1995.

Thomas Hardy, 'The Colour' from *The Complete Poems* by Thomas Hardy, Macmillan.

Michael Harrison, 'In the Stable: Christmas Haiku' from *Junk Mail*, Oxford University Press, courtesy of the author.

Michael Hartnett, 'Sickroom' from *Selected and New Poems* (1994), by kind permission of the author and The Gallery Press.

Seamus Heaney, 'When All the Others' from *The Haw Lantern*, by permission of the author and Faber & Faber.

Cicely Herbert, 'The Juggler's Wife', from 'Strolling Players', 1978.

Rita Ann Higgins, 'Poetry Doesn't Pay', courtesy of the author

Russell Hoban, Small, Smaller' from *The Pedalling Man*, Heinemann, 'Skilly Oogan' from *Six of the Best*, Puffin.

Miroslav Holub, 'The Door' translated by Ian Milner from *Poems: Before and After, Collected English Translations*, Bloodaxe Books, 1990.

Langston Hughes, 'Color' from *Collected Poems* by Langston Hughes. Copyright (c) 1994 by the Estate of Langston Hughes. Reprinted by permission of Alfred A. Knopf Inc.

Ted Hughes, 'Leaves' from *Season Songs*, by permission of Faber & Faber.

Terry Jones 'The Experts', reprinted by permission of Pavilion Books from *The Curse of the Vampire Socks* by Terry Jones.

Nan Joyce, 'The Wild Trabler', courtesy of the author.

Patrick Kavanagh 'A Christmas Childhood' and 'In Memory of My Mother' by kind permission of the Trustees of the Estate of Patrick Kavanagh c/o Peter Fallon, Literary Agent, Loughcrew, Oldcastle, Co. Meath, Ireland.

Dan Keane, 'Waterfall', courtesy of the author.

Brendan Kennelly, 'Poem from a Three-Year-Old' and 'The Stones' from Brendan Kennelly: *A Time for Voices: Selected Poems 1960–1990*, Bloodaxe Books, 1990.

Philip Larkin, 'The North Ship' from *The North Ship*, by permission of Faber & Faber.

Michael Longley, 'Botany' and 'The Daffodils', courtesy of the author.

Lindsay MacRae 'The Richest Poor Man in the Valley' and 'Whose Baby?' from *You Canny Shove Yer Granny Off A Bus!* by Lindsay MacRae (Viking, 1995). Copyright (c) Lindsay MacRae, 1995.

Wes Magee, 'The Woodland Haiku', courtesy of the author; 'Until Gran Died' from *Morning Break and Other Poems*, Cambridge University Press and the author.

Jack Prelutsky, 'What Happens to the Colors?' from *My Parents Think I'm Sleeping*, Greenwillow Books.

James Reeves, 'The Old Wife and the Ghost' from *The Blackbird in the Lilac*, and 'W' from *The Wandering Moon and Other Poems*, courtesy of the author c/o Laura Cecil, Literary Agent.

Theodore Roethke 'The Bat' from *The Collected Poems of Theodore Roethke*, by permission of Faber & Faber.

Gabriel Rosenstock, 'An Breac', 'An Mhuc', 'Snáthaid an Phúca', and 'Teilifís', courtesy of the author.

Clive Samson, 'The Poem I'd Like to Write' from *An English Year*, the author c/o David Higham Associates.

Vernon Scannell, 'Growing Pain' from *New & Selected Poems*, by permission of Robson Books Ltd.; 'Uncle Albert', courtesy of the author.

Norman Silver, 'Changes;' from *The Walkmen Have Landed*, by permission of Faber & Faber.

James Simmons, 'Claudy' from Selected Poems, by kind permission of the author and The Gallery Press.

Gordon Snell, 'William Caxton' from *Hysterically Historical*, Hutchinson.

David Sutton, 'Yobs', copyright David Sutton from *Flints* (1986), reproduced by permission of Peterloo Press.

Matthew Sweeney, 'A Boy' from *Fatso in the Red Suit*, by permission of Faber & Faber.

George Szirtes, 'Dream and Forgetting' translation of poem by Gyözö Ferencz from *The Colonnade of Teeth*, Bloodaxe; 'A Small Girl Swinging' from *Selected Poems 1976–1996*, Oxford University Press; 'Riddles' from *The Red-All-Over Riddle Book*, by permission of Faber & Faber.

Clive Webster 'Acrostic', from *My First Has Gone Bonkers*, Puffin.

Carolyn Wells, Two Tongue Twisters, Puffin.

Colin West, 'Ben' and 'Insides' from *What Would You Do with a Wobble-dee-woo?* Hutchinson.

William Carlos Williams, 'The Horse' and 'The Red Wheelbarrow' from *Collected Poems*, Carcanet Press Ltd.

Kit Wright, 'All of Us' from *Great Snakes* by Kit Wright (Viking, 1994), copyright (c) Kit Wright 1994, 'Charlotte's Dog' from *Cat Among the Pigeons* by Kit Wright (Viking Kestrel, 1987) copyright (c) Kit Wright, 1987, and 'Grandad', courtesy of the author.

William Butler Yeats, 'The Lake of Isle of Innisfree', courtesy of Michael B. Yeats.

Benjamin Zephaniah, 'Dis Fighting', courtesy of the author.

'Traditional Riddles in Irish', 'Ní Raibh Bríste ar bith ag Brian Ó Loinn' from *Cniogaide Cnagaide*, collected by Nicholas Williams, An Clóchomhar, 1988.

'Hey Diddle Diddle'/'Haigh Didil Didil' and 'Ring-a-Ring o' Roses'/'Ring-a-Ring-a-Rósaí' from *Rabhlaí Rabhlaí*, edited by Roibeard Ó Cathasaigh, Aonad Forbartha Curaclaim, Coláiste Mhuire Gan Smál, Ollscoil Luimnigh/Oidhreacht Chorca Dhuibhne, Baile an Fheirtéaraigh, Co. Chiarraí, 1998.

Index of First Lines